The Pony Trap:

Escaping the 1987 SMU Football Death Penalty

By: David Blewett

Tower One Books

Dallas, Texas

For the 1987 SMU Football Team…who never had a chance.

III

www.ThePonyTrap.com

ISBN 978-0-9859883-0-2

"It is convenient to have a system of laws
where everyone is a criminal"

Contents

Introduction

When most people hear the term Death Penalty, they think of some convict put to death for his horrible crime. Victims think of justice served. The condemned profess their innocence. Our government argues that we are all safer with the worst criminals no longer among us. They allege that other criminals will be deterred and therefore avoid committing the violent crimes that are eligible for the penalty.

In the sports world there is a Death Penalty too. The NCAA issues its penalty when a member university's athletic program is found in violation of their rules twice within a five year period. It's only a temporary death though. After serving the two-year penalty, a school is allowed to try to rebuild its sports program, if it can. The NCAA used to argue that the penalty would be a deterrent to other violators, but they no longer make that argument.

Since the NCAA was granted the authority to impose the penalty in 1985, twenty-nine of the thirty Division I universities that have been eligible for the Death Penalty have been spared (fourteen of fifteen in football). The NCAA rarely even investigates schools anymore. They grudgingly respond if the media exposes violations, but for the most part the NCAA has become more interested in running tournaments and protecting their prerogatives.

The one school that did get the penalty was Southern Methodist University (SMU) in 1987. I was a third year defensive end on that team and I experienced the effects of that penalty up close and personal.

The SMU Death Penalty was a marker. It was a date certain when the NCAA grew up and tried to demonstrate its supremacy. The penalty they imposed on us did what its name suggested. It killed our team, it killed our community support, and it killed the energy and enthusiasm that SMU spent decades building.

Younger people are probably unfamiliar with the dominance of SMU Football at different times and specifically from 1980 through 1985. They are likely unaware that we were the winningest program in the country and regularly fought for and won conference and national championships. We were the best team in the country until the NCAA decided to knock us down. On the other side of the argument the NCAA maintained that we broke their rules and deserved to be knocked down.

Whenever I discussed those events, it was inevitable that someone would comment about how SMU players got paid better than the Dallas Cowboys or how SMU was somehow the only school out there that was cheating. They were wrong of course, but I quickly learned we were an easy target and that there was no good rebuttal.

After all this time, I am struck by the durability of that penalty. It still defines the SMU football program. No SMU coaches, players, or boosters from that time period are even around and yet the Death Penalty lives on. It's alive every time another school is accused of a violation. Every time SMU has a good game, a good season, or a bowl invitation...there it is. It's the penalty that never dies. I didn't like it, but after so many years I had gotten used to it.

In 2010 my attitude started to change. I went to a few games with my kids. I started to weigh in on other college football scandals without concern that my own scandal might be a problem. And I started to learn. I learned what SMU had been up to in the last 25 years. I went to Mustang Club luncheons and Lettermen's Association events and I observed what had happened to those groups. I reestablished some old friendships and I met a lot of the new people trying to make the program better than it had been. It was eye opening to say the least.

Looking back on that time, I never got to finish my last two years of playing football at SMU. Every now and then I wondered if I still had eligibility and could play. But that was ridiculous. It was better to just grow up and move on.

Then, two incidents occurred that changed everything for me. One involved a doctor and my health. The other was my daughter and her simple question. Those two events pushed me to dig up the Death Penalty. They pushed me to find out what really happened, and they pushed me to find out if I still had the eligibility to play college football again for SMU.

Chapter One:
February 25, 1987 - Death

It was like the end of a long forced march. We were tired. The morning was overcast and there was a chill in the air. Slowly we arrived and began to gather in groups. There were no smiles or handshakes. We looked to the ground, we kicked at the dirt, and then we haltingly shuffled inside.

We had been ordered to a team meeting at SMU's Ownby Stadium to watch a show. A show about us. The room we were directed to was a room where we had gathered many times over the years to hear motivational speeches from our head coach, or an explanation of recent interactions with the NCAA from our athletic director, or a congratulatory message from our university president. But this morning would be different. It was Wednesday, February 25, 1987. After months of rumors and seemingly endless speculation, it was time to hear our sentence.

There was nothing special about the room. Plenty of chairs for our entire team were arranged in rows facing a low stage. Scattered about the stage were the podium and the miscellaneous audio visual equipment our coaches used to prepare us for any upcoming opponent. Instead of a school official on stage to address us, a closed circuit television had been set up with a direct link to the SMU Student Center where all the action was taking place.

The main feature that made this a desirable place to put us players during today's event was that it was over half a mile from the Student Center. We seventy-one innocent players would not get the chance to face our accuser, nor for that matter, have our accuser face us. There would be no threat of outbursts or verbal exchanges to disrupt the proceedings. Someone had carefully thought this through.

At the Student Center were two hundred plus media types from across the country. Joining them were a few hardy SMU supporters and the three presenters for today's press conference.

Representing SMU were Dr. Lonnie Kliever and Professor William Stallcup. Dr. Kliever was a Professor of Religious Studies and SMU's designated faculty representative on all NCAA matters. He had played a key role in negotiating today's outcome. Professor Stallcup was SMU's interim president due to the recent resignation of our sitting president, L. Donald Shields.

Representing the NCAA was David Berst. He was the Director of NCAA Enforcement and was responsible for the SMU investigation as well as today's report.

At 9:00 a.m. they began their presentation live in the student center. We crowded around our twenty-inch closed-circuit television deep inside Ownby Stadium and struggled to hear what they said. We hung on each word, anticipating something dramatic.

This moment was the end of the most recent investigation of the SMU Football team. It was also the most serious. Since the allegations first broke four months earlier, we had been waiting for this day. Four months of constant and negative press coverage. Four months of watching our coaches, our athletic department staff, and even our university president resign. Four months of listening to Dr. Kliever tell us that he was in charge of SMU's investigation. Four months of listening to him tell us that SMU would disclose everything and beg for mercy from the NCAA. Four months of wondering what the NCAA would do.

Most of us had come to believe that we would be getting the Death Penalty. We hoped we were wrong. After all, we told the NCAA everything and they said self-disclosure would be to our benefit when they issued their penalty. But we knew the NCAA wanted us. They had chased us for a decade with limited success. Was there any way once they had us they would let us go?

No, I thought, *it would be Death*.

The minutes ticked by as we anxiously waited. Finally Berst began. He spoke slowly and mentioned thirteen players who had been paid. He said they had been paid between $50 and $725 per month for a total of $61,000 over a two year period. Some payments occurred after the date the Death Penalty was authorized and SMU was therefore eligible for the penalty.

We knew all that. What was our penalty?

He discussed the long history of SMU football violations and said the NCAA membership demanded harsh penalties for repeat violators.

We knew that too. What was taking so long?

He went on. The NCAA felt that "at least the primary or the fundamental elements of the proscribed penalty be applied in this case."

Fine, but what was our penalty?

Berst looked terrible. He was sweating and turned pale. He was almost there. *Come on* we thought, just a bit more and we would know.

He took a breath. He steadied himself. Then he leaned forward and launched into his closing. "The university will be prohibited from participating in any football game or scrimmage with outside competition in 1987. During the 1988 football season, the university shall be limited to no more than seven games…none of which may be considered a home game." He did it; he killed us.

Berst pushed back from the table as Dr. Kliever began his remarks. He tried to stand but it was too much. He had to get out of there and stumbled a bit as he stepped off the stage. He almost made it to the door when he collapsed.

His disruption only lasted a few minutes. After a short break the SMU representatives continued with their statements. Before they concluded, Berst returned looking determined and took his seat. They moved on to take questions from the reporters, and we moved on to discuss what the penalty meant for us.

We were confused. We expected a full two-year penalty, not a one-year penalty modified without home games in year two. How did that even work? Would our rivals agree to play us in 1988 under those terms? Would new coaches be hired or were we on our own? Were we expected to stay at SMU and just practice for a year or two? Would we lose our eligibility?

It was not clear for those of us that simply wanted to play, but we knew it was bad and that football at SMU had changed forever.

As we accepted the fact that they had killed us, we became angry. Even though we thought we were prepared, the reality of it was shocking. Off color remarks were made and there were many I-told-you-so's. We stomped around and proclaimed how unfair it was. But there were no cameras or media to capture the raw emotion from those of us actually bearing the brunt of the penalty.

We knew telling the NCAA everything was a mistake. We had always known the NCAA as our adversary, would never show mercy. We started to discuss our options immediately. Some said they were going to transfer while others said they could stick out losing just one season. Most of us didn't know what we would do. We had no coaches or athletic staff left to help us or tell us what it all meant.

David Berst of the NCAA was no help. He didn't bother making the short walk to our confined space to explain the penalty or take questions from us. He might have used the excuse that since he passed out during the press conference he wasn't up to talking to us. But we had no way to know because nobody came to tell us anything. Clearly we were on our own.

I have always thought that Berst passing out was a bigger part of the story than we ever knew. The man had given press conferences, played judge, and sentenced numerous schools in his dozen or so years of running enforcement for the NCAA. The man was a professional. Professional assassins do not pass out at the crucial moment. He was too nervous; like he was hiding something or covering up an enormous lie. He said he was suffering from the after-effects of the flu, but I never bought it. What was he hiding that was so disturbing that he passed out in the middle of successfully killing the SMU Mustang Football team? I wondered...

Once the penalty sank in and I fully comprehended what it meant, college took on a whole new perspective. Priorities changed for me. Life looked different. With my football team gone and my career over, I tried to blot it all out and move on.

I graduated and moved around the country a bit before returning to Dallas in the mid-1990's. I got married, had a bunch of kids and set about living my life. I settled in East Dallas a scant two miles from SMU's campus. In fact, I drove by the campus nearly every day, but I was not engaged with SMU athletics and I kept my distance.

As I grew my family, I left all vestiges of playing football behind. I didn't own an SMU shirt. I didn't have an SMU sticker on my car. There was no flag on my house. Yes I was still fairly large and I weighed the same as when I played, but by 2010 my 6'- 4" 275 pound frame was arranged somewhat differently.

I continued to pick up bits and pieces of information about SMU football. There were confidential ramblings over a drink or offhand remarks at a party. But for the most part, I avoided the subject whenever I could and hardly anybody ever inquired as to whether I had played.

I kept up with a few old teammates, but we never discussed what happened. We always talked of other school memories or our lives after school. For us, SMU football was a time that just ended one day. Even if we wanted to talk about it, there was nothing to say. The NCAA and the media had done a great job of tarnishing us. We were all guilty.

Chapter Two:
2010 - Summer in Michigan

It was the summer of 2010 and time for our annual vacation in Upper Michigan. My wife Kristin is from Cincinnati and her family had been vacationing in the Grand Traverse area for thirty years. So it became a normal summer tradition for us to drive twenty-plus hours north to beautiful Crystal Lake and spend a week or two of relaxation with her family.

Leaving the 100+ degree heat back in Dallas was one of the biggest attractions of this destination each year. If we remained in Dallas, we would have had to hide indoors to avoid melting. Whereas on Crystal Lake, the normal temperatures were 75-degree days and 55-degree nights. Unknown to us, that summer was unseasonably warm in upper Michigan. To compound the problem, they didn't have infrastructure to handle 90+ degree heat. Their homes and stores didn't have air conditioning and there was nowhere to hide, day or night. But we didn't know that as we drove north. We took three leisurely days to get there since we were on vacation. The entire drive up we thought of the crisp water and cool evenings awaiting us.

When we arrived we discovered the heat. We expected it to cool off in the evening as it had in years past, but no it remained hot all night long. There wasn't even a breeze stirring to help us sleep. Fortunately, we were on the lake so we could go swimming and cool off. Unfortunately, the water was also warmer than normal and encouraged a higher than normal bacterial infestation. These bacteria caused pimply outbreaks on whatever skin was exposed to them. Apparently they could get inside you too; but we didn't know that then, so we made the best of it.

After a long and miserable 90 degree vacation without air conditioning and away from the scorching Texas heat, we drove back to Dallas as fast as we could. In fact, we drove straight through. Not to get back to Dallas, but to get back to our home and the air-conditioned bliss it offered.

Then it hit me. I didn't feel right. Not sick exactly. Not any pain or discomfort. I just had a case of diarrhea that I couldn't shake. No big deal. I knew it would go away in a day or so.

Nope. Two weeks later I still had it and I started getting concerned. Three weeks later, I started researching my symptoms on the Internet. Four weeks later, I told Kristin that I had cancer.

At this point, I was forty-four years old and hadn't been to a doctor in four years, the main reason being that I was a man and I played football in the 1980's. In playing shape twenty-five years ago, I weighed in at 275 pounds. I ate and drank what I wanted. Now, I weighed about the same at 273 pounds and I figured that I was fine. My wife of course didn't buy any of this. She knew my body had changed and hinted that maybe I should be working out. I kept telling her about being an athlete in the 1980's and therefore didn't need to.

She thought I was an idiot for not going to the doctor after just a few days of diarrhea, much less four weeks. She also thought I was an idiot for not going to a doctor in four years. But, what did she know? She didn't even think I had cancer. I decided to show her. I went to the doctor to get confirmation.

The doctor was a nice enough fellow but he didn't seem too concerned about my cancer. He took my vital signs, did a blood test, inspected my rear, and then asked if I had any problems. I told him about my four miserable weeks of diarrhea and waited for his reaction. Nothing. I tried again. I told him that I had looked up my symptoms on the Internet and was concerned.

"Cancer?" he said.

"Yes." I could tell he finally got it.

Then he said, "Don't look things up on the Internet. It'll say you have cancer every time. See a doctor instead." He looked at me like I was idiot and told me that I should have come in earlier. He also said that I didn't have cancer, but a bacterial infection. Probably from something I ate or drank.

Or swam in I thought...that damn lake in Michigan.

He told me it would get better. However, I was a bit heavy, out of shape, and my cholesterol was through the roof. I wisely decided against telling him about being an athlete. He prescribed something for my high cholesterol then told me to lose some weight. Just like that he was gone.

Silly doctor.

Not only did I not go to doctors, I didn't do prescriptions. Yet fresh off my cancer scare, which nobody but me took seriously, I woke up. That doctor visit gave me just the right shove to get up and do something about my health.

Chapter Three:
2010 - Running

Rather than take drugs to lower my cholesterol, I decided to lose weight and see if that would help. I gave myself six months. And then, if I failed, I would fill the prescription and accept middle age as gracefully as possible.

Like most former athletes, we all think that it comes naturally and takes little to maintain. That is why most former athletes are fat. When I say former athletes, I mean linemen. There were always exceptions to the fat former football players of course. They usually took the form of skilled players such as quarterbacks, wide receivers, and all the other small, fast players that defensive ends like me tried to kill. I still hate those guys. You see them around town. They dropped weight from their playing days, looked great, and then ran marathons. Meanwhile, my buddies and I struggled to keep weight off and usually lost. In my case, it had been gradual. I was able to hide a lot of it on my frame but damn, there was no denying it, I was fat.

I pondered how I would approach getting in shape. Running looked good because I always saw skinny people doing it. I decided it might work for me. I also decided that the first step in starting my workout program was to tell everyone that I was going to work out. This started a guilt reflex so that if I didn't work out, I would be forced to explain why I hadn't. I figured, besides being humiliating, finding a convincing explanation for not working out and then selling it would be harder than actually working out. Therefore, I would work out as the easier of the two options. I was a genius.

By mid-September, I still had my diarrhea problem and that held me back from my plan. I had to get that fixed before starting to get into shape. One of the great things about getting older is that there are many subjects of which you just don't care what other people think. Health problems are one of them. Aging people have problems, they like to talk about them, and they really like to tell you about their solutions. So I began asking around.

With school back in session for my kids, I had a Dad's Club meeting at a local bar. Those Dad's club meetings were great. As responsible parents we cared about our kid's schooling so we got together and drank beer. Yes, we also discussed items we could do for our kids and for upcoming school events all the while swilling beer and gobbling cheese fries. It was there that I began telling all who would listen that I had diarrhea not cancer and that I was "gonna start working out as soon as I got rid of it." I actively sought out answers from my fellow Dad's Club members.

They all seemed uninterested except for one whom I will call Jonathan, because that's his real name. He was very interested in my problem and offered up a solution: fiber. I thought he was drunk, so I ordered another beer and told him again that movement was not the problem. In fact, I would much prefer a lack of movement. He was very serious and said he had been on fiber since the seventh grade and it was awesome. "Clean as a whistle. Bulks up your stool, and will cure diarrhea." I thought about his solution.

Interesting...fight fire with fire.

My philosophy degree from SMU was coming in handy. I finished my cheese fries, had a few more beers, and then went out and bought some fiber. I still don't fully understand how it worked, but within two days of loading up on fiber, my diarrhea was gone. I was clean as a whistle, bulked up, and regular.

It was on to the next step of my master plan: reduce cholesterol while not following the doctor's orders. I figured my problem was that I just ate and drank too much along with not working out. So I would completely change my lifestyle and it would be all better.

I sat in my study thinking about my life to this point. In my twenties, I drank too much hard liquor, so I opted to drink only beer. This got me to my thirties when I met my wife and I discovered red wine. I started drinking wine two times per week, which soon morphed into four to six times per week. I quickly learned that drinking wine was boring without salami and cheese, and of course a heavy dinner around 9:00 pm. For some reason, I started to gain weight. It didn't make any sense. Regardless, I decided to quit drinking alcohol except for special occasions which led to the elimination of my late night salami, cheese, and heavy dinners.

My workouts followed the exact opposite track as my diet. In my twenties, I worked out hard to drop from my football weight of 275 pounds to a leaner 245 pounds. I lifted lighter weights with higher repetitions and ran three times a week. I remember feeling great. In my thirties, I decided I didn't need to lift weights anymore and running three times a week was a bit too much. I thought I could maintain my body by working out only once in a while. So I stopped completely.

I slowly started gaining a few pounds per year but that was normal for a man in his thirties. This trend continued until I was thirty-eight years old and back up to my 1980's football weight of 275 pound without any of those annoying, difficult to maintain muscles. I held that weight for the better part of a decade. I was in my mid-forties when my cholesterol crested over 300. It was time to take action on my running plan.

I contemplated which part of the day I could actually work out. We have a large and young family. My wife has been diligent about getting up before the kids and working out. I thought that was crazy. She could have been sleeping. But she goes non-stop all day until she drops right after the kids go to bed at around 9:00 pm. She had no other option. There was no way I could get up early and run like she did. I'm not a morning guy and it seemed responsible to have one of us home with the kids. I also thought it would be selfish to work out in the evenings when we had dinner and homework and family time. So, I decided to work out in the late evenings when everyone else was asleep.

It was 9:30 pm, September 15, 2010. My family was in bed and I was up alone. This was it. Time to run. I had always been a night owl so I quietly laced up my shoes and went outside for a run. It had been so long since I ran or worked out I literally had no idea what I was going to do. I just knew that since I told so many people about my working out, I had to start. That first run took me one mile down the road before I was too exhausted to continue. I walked slowly back home, out of breath.

But the next night, there I was, at it again. And the next night, and the next night too. I decided to jog and walk until I could jog for real distance. After a few weeks, I was jogging pretty well and felt good doing it. Then the pain kicked in. At about the three mile distance, my knees began to ache. I hurt my knee twice in college and it still bothered me a bit. I was simply too heavy to run any long distance pain free. My dilemma was a common one. I needed to lose weight to be able to run without pain, and I needed to run to be able to lose weight. I kept at it.

In mid-October, I was bragging about my efforts to a neighbor who was a big runner. He was a marathoner and not impressed in the least. I tried the old "I'm not built like you" angle. He didn't care, though he did offer some advice. He told me I was a heel striker, and that jogging in that manner transferred the shock of running directly from my heel up to my knee. This caused my knee pain. He showed me how to run on the balls of my feet by only lightly touching my heel to the ground after the front part of my foot had touched. He said to run so that someone watching me run towards him would not be able to see the bottom of my shoe.

The first time I tried his advice, I ran six miles without knee pain. Two weeks later I was up to twelve miles, still without pain. Surprisingly, I had also lost ten pounds.

Now that I could run a decent distance, I was bored. I needed a goal. This running thing was easy. I decided to run the Dallas White Rock Marathon on December 5, only six weeks away.

I stuck to my usual plan of telling people what I was going to do, to force myself to actually do it. I started telling people I was going to run the marathon. First up was my wife. She said I would never make it starting this close to the race. My best friend also said I wouldn't make it. I was crushed. Joel had known me for almost thirty years. How could he doubt me?

"Easy," he said.

Ok, now I was pissed. I really was going to run the marathon, even if it caused structural damage.

Each night, I continued to run at Glencoe Park about a half mile from my house. I would leave about 9:30 pm, run to the park, and then run the approximately half-mile track around the park until I was tired. Usually, when I started there were softball games going on. They would finish up around 11:00 pm and I would continue on alone, adding distance each time. In November, I was up to sixteen miles and my runs were taking longer. Running at Glencoe Park made my wife nervous. It was a normal Dallas park, and safer than most. They found only one, maybe two bodies max in the ten years I had lived in the neighborhood. I figured it was highly unlikely I would get killed. I told Kristin that there were lights and softball games so it was safe. Then one night as I was doing a long run, the lights went out. It was 11:30 pm. At first I didn't understand, and then I got it. The games were over by then and Dallas was broke. They were doing taxpayers like me a favor by shutting off the lights and saving electricity. At the time, I didn't consider it a favor.

It was odd running in the dark, all alone, at midnight. It was odder still when the homeless took up residence on their park benches at 12:30 am. Around and around the half-mile loop I would go, sometimes past 2:00 am. I would be running past the dazed homeless people lap after lap. They never said "Hi," and I never stopped to chat. They just silently watched me and thought I was the crazy one.

A great friend, Johnny Delavaldene, lived in a house right on White Rock Lake. He had run a few marathons and offered to run with me on some long training runs around the lake. We met a couple of times a week as I got closer to the race. We ran and talked. His encouragement really helped me break the twenty and twenty-four mile markers. On race day, he was in front of his house at mile eighteen making sure I didn't quit.

The morning of the race I weighed myself…240 pounds. I had lost over thirty pounds in ten weeks. I didn't have time to train properly and never got a marathon length training run. This would be my longest run. I was a bit nervous, but I told everyone I was going to do it so I had to go.

I ran the marathon and finished in 4 hours 57 minutes. I didn't set any land speed records and towards the end, my three-year-old could have walked faster than I was running. But I never stopped except for water. I did it. I made it to the end. Kristin was there shouting encouragement and jogging the last mile with me, backwards and in cowboy boots. My best friend Joel was there to check on me at miles twelve and fifteen, twenty and twenty-two. I don't know how he kept popping up at the different mile markers. Even though he says he was trying to support me, I was pretty sure he was just making sure I wasn't cheating.

As I crossed the finish line, I thanked God I was still alive. It felt like I was in a car accident. Everything hurt. Running was more physical than I ever realized, but I think the mental part of it was even harder. I knew that if I stopped I would not be able to make myself start again.

Then the post-race shock hit me and I couldn't control my shaking and shivering. I was completely drained of fuel. My wife had to cover me with blankets until I could create enough energy to heat my body again.

After the race people kept asking if I was addicted and if I would continue to run marathons. The answer was an emphatic *no*. It hurt. The magical sensation, the euphoria they say you'll feel as you cross the finish line is nothing but a lie. Runners are crazy. I'm a football player. Or at least I was in the 1980's.

With the marathon out of the way, I made my way home looking forward to a long nap on the couch. I decided to heal, rest up in December, and strictly focus on my diet to keep the weight off through the upcoming holiday season. Then, something happened that pushed me off in an unexpected direction. My SMU past came back. Unlike the hushed quiet conversations amongst us former players, there would be no chance to suppress this. It was on national TV. It was right after the Heisman Trophy presentation. And everyone was talking about it.

Chapter Four:
Amanda's Question

I heard a noise but couldn't decide where it was coming from. My mind was a little off. I opened my eyes and looked at the ceiling. The noise continued. Within seconds I understood that I was lying on my couch and my cell phone was ringing on the table next to me. As I reached for the phone, every single part of my body ached from the marathon two hours earlier.

"Hullo?"

"Dave, I saw it. Do you want to hear?" It was a friend from my SMU days.

"Was it bad?"

"Well...it wasn't good, if that's what you meant. Did I catch you at a bad time?"

"Yeah. I just ran the marathon and I'm napping. I forgot to put my phone on mute. Let me talk to you later."

"Sure Dave...get feeling better."

My friend was talking about the event that happened the previous night. It was an invitation-only private screening of an ESPN documentary on SMU and the Death Penalty. Its title was *Pony Excess*, a play on the Pony Express moniker from the late seventies and early eighties when SMU began to dominate college football again. Thaddeus Matula, a young

SMU grad and filmmaker, was chosen to tell the story. The documentary was part of a "30 for 30" series of films to celebrate the thirty biggest sporting events in the last thirty years ESPN had been in business.

The private showing had been held at the Lakewood Theater in East Dallas. I was invited to attend. I declined but several of my friends went. I learned that the first public airing on TV would be the next Saturday, December 11 immediately following the Heisman Trophy award show on ESPN. The SMU story was considered to be one of the most important of the thirty events and Thad's film was given this coveted spot for its premier. Obviously ESPN hoped for a huge audience to stay tuned and watch. As for me, I thought I might catch it then or I might record it and watch it later.

I knew all about the documentary. Thad called me the previous summer to be in it. I never called him back. I had my fill of interviews back in that time and saw no reason to revisit it. But then I ran into him in October. He walked up to me in Annapolis, Maryland.

"So you're Dave Blewett"

It was a statement and not a question. There I was at the October 16, 2010 SMU v. Navy football game with a bunch of my college buddies for our annual guys trip. Specifically, I was at the Mustang Club pre-game tailgate event and even more specifically, I was at the keg re-filling my beer. My friends and I had never traveled to an SMU game before but decided it was time to start. In our mid-forties, our trips had steadily diminished in excitement; from three weeks in the Greek islands, to five days in Mexico, to now three days in Annapolis. This trip wasn't as elaborate as some of our earlier trips like that Greece trip but we were all married now. We had kids and definitely lacked the energy for a trip like that. This trip was a three day venture centered on the SMU football game but Blue Crabs and the traditions of Annapolis were nice draws too.

Navy was a fun team to watch and their community represented everything that made America great. They had class, they were polite, and they were very appreciative of fans like us who made the trip out there. Their triple option offense was a throw-back to the past and most teams had trouble defending against it. Including SMU. But back in the 1960's, there were some memorable games that SMU won. For example, in 1963 Navy was picked to win the national championship and was led by future hall of famer and Heisman Trophy winner Roger Staubach. SMU was picked to have a mediocre season. The game went back and forth with both teams playing well. Staubach went to the bench twice with a dislocated shoulder. In an aerial battle, SMU took the lead with just over two minutes to play and hung on for the improbable 32-28 victory. Recently, Navy had SMU's number and had won the last two games. But we were hopeful as all current Mustang fans have to be.

He repeated himself. "I said, so you're Dave Blewett."

I was wearing a nametag…and I was looking at a guy with his own nametag that read "Thad Matula." Name seemed vaguely familiar. He says, "I left two messages for you…you never called back. I'm the guy that's making the documentary 'Pony Excess.' Why didn't you call me back?"

My friends who overheard the question looked at me. Thad looked at me. Why didn't I call him back? I stumbled and fumbled through a terrible answer; something about being busy and meaning to call. I think Thad walked off while I was still talking. My friends didn't walk off, and they wanted a better answer. They didn't know anything about a documentary on SMU Football being made and they were curious. They knew I played football at SMU in the mid-eighties. They knew I was there three years prior to the Death Penalty and then stayed two years after to graduate. I knew every detail of that event, and yet I wanted no part of his film.

When the December 11, 2010 premier of Thad's film came, I passed on watching it but I did record it. I wasn't real busy. I just decided the time wasn't right for me. Over the next few weeks the raw emotion of the events presented in his film came back. At Christmas parties hosted by my SMU friends, talk was dominated by the Death Penalty again and that ESPN documentary. It was intense. Many people asked if I had seen it and I had to confess I had not. I stood and listened to people rail about the NCAA and WFAA for hounding us while everybody else was cheating just as badly back then. Dale Hansen, the local sports reporter with WFAA who supposedly broke the story was the hated guy who brought it all down.

I voiced some opinions but for the most part didn't say much. What could I say? I knew what happened because I was there. Since I hadn't seen the documentary I didn't know what to add. I didn't hate Dale Hansen or WFAA and I was just surprised at the animosity coming from SMU grads that never played football or got hurt by the penalty. They were hot. Many of those folks were younger than me and experienced a school and a degree that was weakened by the entire episode. I never paid attention to how the regular students were harmed back then. But during that Christmas party season, I experienced the anger and the pain that lingered after all that time.

In late December, I still hadn't found a convenient time to watch the documentary. Then one day, my oldest daughter Amanda came up and asked me some questions.

"Dad, did you play football at SMU?"

I previously discussed with my kids that I had gone to SMU but I rarely mentioned playing football. In fact, I rarely watched football on TV. So in reality, my children didn't know much about that part of my life.

I looked down and saw her eyes. There appeared to be some concern. A feeling in my gut told me I was about to go down a road I had hoped to avoid.

"Yes, I played football at SMU. Why baby…what did you hear?"

Amanda scrunched up her face and said, "I heard something bad happened there...Daddy, did you do anything wrong?"

So that was it. Someone at school had told her about her dear old dad and his cheatin' days at SMU. My fuse was instantly lit. Amanda probably sensed it. "Yes, some bad things happened. What did you hear?"

"I just heard some things." Amanda immediately shut down. I could not get her to tell me what it was she heard, but I didn't press too hard. I wondered how long it would take, how many years it would be before I could put this behind me. But then I realized it would never go away. College football had gotten even bigger than it was in the 1980's. The money flowing into college football was exploding, and with the increased money and pressure to win there was a continuous stream of sports scandals since the SMU penalty.

Even though many of the newer scandals eclipsed SMU's, let's face it, the granddaddy college scandal of them all was still the 1987 SMU Football scandal. Every disgrace would be measured against us, and not just the money scandals. Any college scandal where the NCAA was involved and where there could be potentially serious penalties would reference us. We were set up as the benchmark in NCAA infractions and there was no way out for us.

When was I going to stop avoiding all of this? Wasn't it time to air it all out?

Yes I decided...it was time.

I told my daughter the truth. I told her it was a complex story and that I would answer any questions she had. I told her I wanted to show something to her as I grabbed the remote control and turned on the TV. Before we could start my wife Kristin came into the room. She had been listening to the exchange between me and Amanda and wanted to join us.

Kristin was nine years younger than me and had never asked about my football playing days. Frankly, I don't think she cared if I ever played football. And since she was from

24

Cincinnati in the days before the Internet and instant global communications, she never really understood the details of the Death Penalty. She truly had no idea how big SMU football was until she moved to Dallas in 1996.

So with my wife on one side and my daughter on the other, we settled in to watch Thad's film *Pony Excess* and the end of my football career.

Chapter Five:
Cherry Creek

I was 6'- 4'' when I was thirteen years old and every-thing hurt. My feet hurt when I walked. My knees and ankles throbbed. I was working on a crop of acne, which was com-ing in just fine. Let's face it: nobody really likes adolescence when all these strange things happen to your body, especially when you are the new kid in school which of course, I was. In summary: I was tall, uncoordinated, in pain, with acne and no friends…yes, those were good times.

My parents thought playing football would solve all of my problems. I made the second string of the "B" team on the Cherry Creek High School freshman team and this was not helpful. Cherry Creek, in Southeast Denver, Colorado was and still is a fantastic school. It was large with around 1,000 students per grade and offered great academics along with every sport and club you could imagine. My freshman year was a tough one, but luckily I stopped growing which meant my body had time to get accustomed to my size. By the time I was a sophomore, I was the starting left tackle on our "A" team, I had made a handful of great friends, and things were looking up.

Football at Creek was very competitive. Lots of kids tried out. They had great coaches and facilities. Most of the players on the teams had played together since Pop Warner and they knew how to win. During my sophomore year we lost only one game. It was to Smoky Hill High School and it was only because our starting quarterback, Chris Rule, moved up to Varsity. After that loss, he asked to come back down to lead our team. With Chris back as quarterback, we won every game the rest of the season. In fact, we beat most of our opponents by twenty points or more. My junior year on varsity, we continued winning and were undefeated as Colorado State Champions.

The summer between my junior and senior years I had the good fortune to be offered a job on a cattle ranch in Wyoming to put up barbed wire fence, brand yearlings, and train for football. The *Pride of Wyoming Ranch* in Wheatland, Wyoming was a short five-hour drive north of Denver and in the middle of nowhere. My best friend's dad, Dave Cronk, owned the ranch and offered four of us jobs. The offer was simple: work hard for ten bucks a day without any distraction from girls or parties or fun. I jumped at the opportunity.

Each day we got up and went out to some rock-hard stretch of nothing where a cow would never wander and dug holes to stick posts in, to which we would attach barbed wire for a fence that would never see a cow. On special days we got to brand, castrate, and immunize three hundred pound yearlings. At the end of a long day we would ride in the back of the truck to our bunkhouse, relaxing in the truck bed as best we could with the bumps tossing us about. On most days our foreman/trainer would stop the truck, make us get out and then throw our running shoes out the window. There was nothing like a dusty three-mile run home as the coyotes came out howling and sniffing around for their dinner.

Home for us was a bunkhouse that Mr. Cronk had Gold's Gym supply. There were more weights and racks than beds and chairs. He stocked multiple freezers with hundreds of pounds of meat and comfort foods. So our daily routine was to eat a lot, build fences, eat more, then run and lift weights, and then eat even more. At some point we went to bed where morning quickly came and we did it all over again. In two months, we all grew significantly bigger and stronger.

On Saturday nights, we went into town and cruised up and down the main drag looking for anything to do. We bought cheap beer. We hit on the local ladies. And then we went home to our bunkhouse, alone but for the coyotes.

At the beginning of August it was time to head back down to Denver and the beginning of football practice. At Creek they had a test to determine your athleticism and to see if you worked out over the summer months. It was called the A.C.T. test and it was composed of four strength tests and four speed tests, each worth ten points for a potential of eighty points. This formula made it hard for big linemen to have any advantage over smaller skilled players. Within the test they had a club for those able to break seventy points. The guys who typically made the club were the fullbacks and the linebackers who were both strong and fast.

As a 6'4" 225 pound junior, I scored thirty-six points. It was pretty average and nobody was impressed. After the ranch experience, I was 6'4" and weighed 245 pounds. I now benched over 300 pounds, squatted over 400 pounds, ran a 4.9 forty-yard dash, and scored a 71 on the A.C.T. I was the only lineman to make the elite "70 Club" and was now ready for my senior year.

Cherry Creek was coached by Fred Tesone. He had coached Creek to a great win-loss record over the previous twenty years and was an institution within Colorado high school football. But Creek had brought home only one state championship during his tenure. In 1982, my junior season we were undefeated and first time state champions.

Now in my senior year, we returned an even better team and expected to repeat. We did. My senior team went undefeated again and averaged over six yards per play of offense and thirty-six points per game. Our defense was dominant as well and allowed only ten points and 150 yards per game. We won our second straight Colorado State Championship, we were ranked as the 8th best team in the nation, and sixteen of our twenty-two starters got scholarships to play Division I football. That team was inducted into the Colorado State High School Hall of Fame in 2012.

After an incredibly fun and successful high school football experience, it was time to leave Cherry Creek and head to college. But where to go?

In recent years, National Signing Day has been the first Wednesday in February. Back in the 1980's, it was the second Wednesday and I needed that extra week. It was great that we were undefeated and had won the state championship again, but it meant our season lasted an extra month through early December. Therefore, I only had eight weeks to look at and decide which college to attend with the Christmas holidays taking up a good chunk of that time.

Coach Tesone had gone through the college recruiting process numerous times with many of his former players. He also had five sons who were great athletes and had been recruited. He didn't like the distraction of the process so he restricted it until after a season was over. I read in the newspapers that certain colleges were interested in me but I had no idea how serious they were. The week after our state championship, Coach Tesone called me to his office and gave me a box with letters from colleges all over the country. I was shocked.

College coaches only had thirty scholarships in a given year to hand out. They had to be careful to make sure they used them wisely so they spent a ton of time evaluating top players from selected high schools. Athletes also spent a lot of time checking out colleges hoping to be offered scholarships to their preferred schools. I grew up in California, Arizona, and recently Colorado. I did not grow up with a team that was "my team." I was also a late bloomer and did not get recruited prior to my senior year. As of December 10,

I had not talked to a single school and had to decide fast which ones to consider.

Chapter Six:
Choosing SMU

To say my recruiting process was frantic would be an understatement. I was recruited by all of the Western Athletic Conference schools, most of the Big Eight Schools, a few of the Pac-10 schools, a couple of the Southeastern Conference schools, and one school from the Southwest Conference: SMU. I never really looked at most of those schools because I liked the idea of staying close to home so my family could watch me play. Through Dave Cronk's ranch and my experiences in Wyoming, I had to consider the Cowboy's. Most of the guys on my high school team were committing to Colorado State, so that was attractive. I liked the idea of playing in the Big Eight against some of the best schools in the country, so that made the University of Colorado a top contender. Other schools around the country were too far away or the value of their degree just wasn't there.

In 1984, the University of Colorado was rebuilding. Coach Bill McCartney arrived in 1982 to turn around a 1-10 team and promised to do it with Colorado kids, many of whom I already knew. Coach McCartney was a Christian and loudly professed his Christianity in my parent's living room. He talked about his relationship with God being first in his life and forcefully told me and my parents that winning football games was secondary. He promised to be a good shepherd over me if I chose to come to Colorado.

I liked Coach McCartney. He was a good coach and seemed like a good man. I really liked his thoughts on rebuilding the team with Colorado high school kids. As we got closer to signing day, I was more and more sure that the University of Colorado was it. Then I started reading in the newspapers about numerous Junior College transfers and California high school kids committing to Colorado. I didn't know any of the players who were committing and started thinking hard about my choice. They were a struggling team and their proximity and the chance to play with existing friends were the only real draws.

On the other hand there was Southern Methodist University. SMU was the most successful college football program in the country from 1981 to 1984. They beat everybody. Up in Colorado we rarely got to see them on TV, but everyone who followed college football talked about Eric Dickerson, Craig James, Lance McIlhenny, and Michael Carter. The Pony Express was big time. As I waffled about CU and their promises, I started to consider the idea of going to the proven SMU program even though it was eight hundred miles away in Dallas.

I told my recruiting coach, Whitey Jordan, I was getting warm to the idea of SMU. I told my mom I was thinking of SMU and she counseled me that a "private school education was always worth more than a public school education." Then I got a call from David Richards. David had committed early to SMU and was calling to help shore up the recruiting class. He was 6'-5" and 325 pounds. He was fast and coordinated at a time when 300-pound linemen had yet to appear in the NFL. He won every award a high school athlete could get and was considered the number one recruit in the nation. I knew who he was all right.

David and I chatted on the phone. He helped me understand a bit more about Dallas and what SMU was in Dallas.

SMU was a winner now and did not need to rebuild. I was excited. It would cost me to go so far away to play. The proven SMU team did not have many spots for incoming freshmen to play. I could play faster at a lesser school, but I liked the idea of being on a winner like my high school team was. I thought I could handle the trade-off of having to struggle to earn a spot with a winning team as opposed to playing earlier on a struggling team. Once I decided that education and a winning program trumped proximity, I decided to go to SMU.

I never called CU or any of the other schools back. I just told the newspapers that I had committed to SMU and that was the end of that. Later, I heard through the grapevine that the CU coaches were shocked; they thought they had me. It was the California Junior College transfers and the lies about them. I didn't know what else I could believe and chose to move on.

National Signing Day was a big deal. At Cherry Creek we had sixteen players committing so it was particularly exciting and busy. Parents and Media were present. Coaches were everywhere. They flew in, signed a kid, and then flew on to the next school. Some kids simply signed their Letters of Intent and faxed them in. Confirmation phone calls from head coaches signified an accepted deal. My recruiting coach from SMU, Whitey Jordan, flew to Denver, signed me, and then he was off...back to Texas to sign a Houston player. It was fast, it was exciting, and then it was official. I was a Mustang and the only player SMU recruited or signed from Colorado.

I chose SMU because it was a private school that had pretty girls, cool uniforms, played in Texas Stadium, was a member of the elite SWC, and was a winner. But I really didn't know much about Texas, much less Dallas. I knew Dallas was called "Big D" because they did everything big. There was a television show that made it seem glamorous. It was the kind of place where everything seemed possible.

Recent graduates from all over the country poured in. Money was being printed, the city was growing in every direction, and SMU was in the heart of it all. I couldn't wait to get there and grab my part of it.

I worked out through the summer getting ready to leave my home in Colorado to play college football some place down in Texas. Two weeks before I was set to leave and travel to SMU for two-a-days practice, I came down with mono. Almost overnight I lost fifteen pounds. But I didn't worry because I was eighteen and bulletproof.

Undeterred, in August I packed my 1976 Bicentennial Edition International Harvester Scoutermobile, perhaps the finest piece of machinery ever produced by man. It was otherwise known as a 1976 beat up Scout II with no air conditioning, cruise control, or adjustable seats. It was paid for, got nine miles to the gallon, and had a top speed of around 65 mph. I waved goodbye to Denver and drove to my new life in Dallas.

As I drove south I began to have doubts. There were no interstate highways connecting Denver to Dallas. The best way to drive it then was the same as how you drive it today. You drove straight down I-25 to New Mexico, hung a left on some state highway and headed into Texas. Soon, I found that there were no trees in large parts of Texas and that it was really big, like a whole 'nother country. The further south I traveled the more desolate it got.

The panhandle of Texas in August was hot, flat, and seemed to go on forever. In an airplane, it looked like there were lots of lakes and rivers. On the ground I didn't see any. I had only been to Texas one time. The weather in January during my recruiting trip to SMU was great. What I didn't know then but was learning now, was that Texas in August was hell on earth.

I had the windows down like normal in Colorado. But the Texas air was not refreshing. It felt like a blast furnace. Rolling up the windows created an oven. I was trapped between the blast furnace and the oven. I chose the blast furnace. Hundreds of miles later in my old Scout with no air conditioning, and no cruise control or adjustable seats, I started thinking about the University of Colorado in Boulder. It was only a short thirty miles from home in the much cooler foothills of the Colorado Rocky Mountains. It was a nice fantasy but it was too late to turn around.

By the time I got to Dallas I'm sure my skin had changed texture and I had lost another ten pounds. I arrived just a couple of hours before our first practice.

Poor planning.

I had no idea Texas was so damn big. The coaches were very sympathetic to my drive and my health condition and said, "Practice is in two hours. Make sure you are there."

I was there and it didn't go well. First of all, I had never experienced heat like this. Second of all, I was used to being one of the biggest, if not *the* biggest guy on the field. I had heard everything was bigger in Texas but this was ridiculous. I was average at best and with the loss of fifteen pounds right before two-a-days, I was behind the eight ball. I really needed those pounds back. (A side note of interest: it is impossible to gain weight in Texas in August while practicing in full football pads two times each day). We worked out and I gradually felt that I could at least hold my own with the other players. But I noticed something, the team seemed small. Not small in size. I mean numbers small. Something was going on because we were missing a lot of players. I had more players on my high school team. I looked around and saw a few other players were concerned as well. I wondered if something had happened. Had we lost over half of our team? If so, where did they go? It wasn't long before I found out the answer and I didn't like it.

Chapter Seven:
1984 Season

I stood on the practice field counting the number of players at this first practice. There were a meager forty or so of us while my high school team had over a hundred. Surely a college program as big as SMU had more than forty players? Tell me I didn't make a mistake coming here.

Within a few minutes, I discovered the reason why our numbers were so low. We were all freshmen. While that explained why there were so few of us, we competed hard and beat each other up pretty good. The next week things got worse. The even bigger upperclassmen arrived and really beat us up. As All-American and All-State recruits from around the country we thought we were great. By the time the upperclassmen were done with us, that was no longer an issue. We all knew where we fell in the pecking order and I'm certain that was by design.

Our 1984 SMU recruiting class was ranked as the 22nd best in the country. There were twenty-eight scholarship players. Most were from Texas but eight of us were from outside the state. The Pony Express phenomenon was starting to allow SMU to recruit nationally and they used that to their advantage in a big way. Most schools back then were only able to recruit regionally. Notre Dame and selected other colleges were able to go national and now SMU was trying. Prior classes had been almost exclusively Texas-based. There was nothing wrong with Texas players, but eight of the nine Southwest Conference schools were in Texas and they were constantly tripping over each other every year in recruiting. A lot of the animosity between the teams stemmed from those recruiting rivalries before a season even began. SMU recognized this and was making a strong push to break out of the pack.

Besides David Richards, the next best offensive lineman of the 1984 recruiting class was Sean Stopperich. He was from Muse, Pennsylvania outside Pittsburgh. He had a different frame than Richards. Dave was big, mountain man big. Sean was big too, 6'- 4'and 275 pounds. But his build was more along the lines of a bodybuilder. On the college and pro football fields bodybuilders didn't have a chance. They were strong, but brittle. Big, but slow. I'm sure Sean was a great high school player, but he had hurt his knee wrestling before his senior year of football. He had surgery and never really showed any mobility while at SMU. Consequently, he got real down on himself.

Sean and David roomed together and became fast friends. As it became obvious that David was going to start and Sean was going to redshirt on the scout team, Sean's depression got worse. He talked of going home back to Pennsylvania. But an SMU booster had moved his family down to Dallas; SMU boosters had also helped his parents lease an apartment and secured jobs for them. Regardless of how unhappy he was becoming, he couldn't just up and leave SMU to go to another school. Sean had a problem.

Things were getting so bad on the field that he couldn't handle it. He asked to be released from his commitment letter so he could return home and try to play football for Pittsburgh. SMU refused and explained the NCAA rules that once he signed his letter SMU had the rights to him for a year. He couldn't transfer without having to sit out a year. Further, since classes had already started he would have to sit out an additional year. By leaving SMU after classes had begun Sean would have to sit out both the 1984 and 1985 seasons. But if SMU released him, then he would only have to sit out the 1984 season. Sean hoped SMU would give in.

It was hard for all of us and particularly hard for those of us from out of state, but Sean never really tried. After two months, on October 8 he left. Sean and his family packed up and went back to Pennsylvania. He quit in the dark of night and he never even tried to explain why or give the coaches a chance to help. He didn't call Coach Collins. He didn't tell me or David or any other players that I know of. He just left. Then he threatened to turn SMU in to the NCAA for monies he and his family had received from the booster who helped them move to Dallas. SMU had to sign his release or else. SMU again refused.

Ultimately, SMU did not sign the release and Sean did sit out those two years. He followed through with his threat and called the NCAA to tell them everything he could about his SMU recruiting experience.

With Stopperich gone and his allegations freshly added to an already open NCAA investigation, those of us that stayed kept working hard. Our upperclassmen had experience but we had lost fifteen senior starters from the 1983 team. 1984 was considered a rebuilding year. Over the summer workouts, the average upper-class player gained ten pounds of "good" weight. Every eligible player from last year's roster was healthy. Counting us freshmen and a handful of walkons, we had 112 players on our roster. Things were looking pretty good.

The team was ranked #12 at the end of last season after a disappointing bowl loss to Alabama and had dropped to preseason #15. But we still expected a good year. Maybe not as good as 1982 or 1983, but a good year. The old Pony Express was to be continued under a new group of starters. Quarterback Lance McIlhenny, an absolute master running the option, was replaced by Junior Don King. King was a standout quarterback out of Dallas Kimball High School who watched as the Ponies rolled through the '82 and '83 seasons. 1984 was his turn. He was different from Lance, faster and more of a runner. Behind him were Reggie Dupard and Jeff Atkins as dual tailbacks. The offensive line was as good as it had ever been. On the defensive front, Michael Carter had been replaced by Jerry Ball. Linebackers were led by 1983 all-conference Anthony Beverly. Although our depth chart only showed two starters returning, most of the players had seen considerable playing time. We were viewed as solid even if we were un-tested.

We opened our season late, September 15 at Louisville and won handily 41-7. Next up was a victory over North Texas and then unbeaten TCU came to Texas Stadium September 29. The rivalry was one sided recently as SMU had beaten TCU every year since 1971. The last time both teams met unbeaten was a 1935 SMU victory when both went 12-1 with SMU as National Champion playing in the Rose Bowl and TCU playing in the Sugar Bowl. We won again 26-17.

Our new offense really came together. King was handling the option well and backs Dupard and Atkins were gaining tremendous yardage. But it was a new wrinkle that Coach Collins added that really confused defenses. The wrinkle was Ron Morris, a wide receiver with 4.4 speed. Morris would trail all the way across the field to catch a pitch option if King didn't keep it or hand off to one of the backs. Collins called it an "Isolation Option." It was devastating. Nobody could stop it. Against TCU he had seven option pitches for fifty-three yards and a touchdown. Ron Morris was becoming a star. We moved up in the rankings to #10 after the TCU win and then traveled to Baylor October 13 to meet the struggling Bears. We won 24-20 and moved up to #7. October 20 we lost to Houston 20-29 and dropped to #14.

October 27 we traveled to Austin to meet the unbeaten and #3 ranked Texas Longhorns. Neither team dominated the other and it could have gone either way. Our offense couldn't move the ball; we had numerous dropped passes, missed two field goals, and were held to a season low 221 yards. Late in the game as we were driving, officials missed a clear pass interference call on fourth down that ended our last chance for victory. We lost 13-7 and dropped to #19. We were still playing well enough for a shot at the conference championship and a postseason bowl but our season was slipping away.

The Aggies came to Dallas after those two losses. We had not lost two regular season games since 1980. This was a big game and make or break for a successful year. Coach Jackie Sherrill had his Aggies ready to go and they quickly punched us in the face. After the first half A&M was up 20-7. In the locker room Coach Collins told us that our season was on the line, and that we were a better team than we showed in the first half. It was gut check time.

His speech worked. It was a different SMU team that took the field in the second half. We racked up 248 yards and scored on three consecutive possessions to take a 28-20 lead. Our defense stepped up and held them to fourteen total yards the rest of the game. People who don't understand how important emotion and honor are to a team would not understand how the right locker room speech can motivate a team to play their best. Collins' speech worked. There were two completely different games in the first and second halves. We recovered in time and pulled out the win.

We won our remaining games with only a close one against Arkansas. We were 9-2 and won the conference for the 3rd time in four years. The Aloha Bowl selected us and we got to whip up on Notre Dame to complete a nice season finishing 10-2 with a final ranking of #8.

After my first year at SMU I took inventory. I had red-shirted that season along with most of the twenty-eight freshmen in our class practicing and preparing for our turn. But as I watched our team play, I salivated thinking how good we would be next year. I continued to work out doing everything I could to get in the best shape possible. My second year of playing college football was right around the corner and I wanted to be ready. This was Division I football in the Southwest Conference. I knew I would be tested and wanted to be big enough and strong enough for the pounding I would take.

Meanwhile, in the background the NCCA continued their investigation, winding their way through the details, grinding ever closer. We knew they were investigating Stopperich but we figured it was no big deal and would not have any serious effect on our continued success. We were wrong.

Chapter Eight:
2011 - Deciding to Play Again

In early January 2011, the dust was settling from ESPN's SMU Death Penalty revival show. My wife and daughter now knew some of the details about what went on at SMU during my playing days. They didn't ask any more questions but I was unsatisfied. My daughter had questioned my integrity. I showed her a film. It wasn't good enough.

Thad had done a good job. The film did explore the endemic nature of the payment systems throughout the Southwest Conference and it touched on why SMU was an easier target than the larger state schools. But there was no backstory, no probing of the NCAA and the underlying reasons why all this happened. He would have needed another two hours to fit it all in.

I saw the anger and bitterness from SMU alums that were chafing at the unfairness of selecting SMU as the worst violator in college football. I was still not fully dialed into everything they were feeling, but I was beginning to understand the anger of being labeled a cheater and not having a response. How could I better respond to my daughter's question?

On the health front, I recovered from my marathon adventure and decided that it would be a waste to lose all the progress I made training for it. So I called up my friend Johnny, the one who encouraged me during the race, and asked if he wanted to occasionally run around the lake. It was approximately nine miles around and was the perfect distance to maintain my shape. He agreed and we began our weekly maintenance runs.

During those runs we solved all the world's problems and discussed all the things we wanted to do with the rest of our lives. Johnny was a fraternity brother, we were good friends, and we naturally ribbed each other as we ran. He was a physical guy and has owned gyms and managed MMA fighters. We discussed the SMU Pony Excess documentary, SMU football in general, and if it would ever be what it was when we were in school. On one of those runs I made some snappy comments about still having eligibility post-Death Penalty and maybe I should, "go out for the team." We laughed about the idea of a 45-year-old guy who had just barely finished a marathon playing Division I football again.

I said something about being in pretty good shape for being able to run the marathon but I was in better shape in the 80's when I was a football player. Johnny laughed harder and said he remembered me from the 80's and that I wasn't in great shape back then…I had just been bigger. He said I was in better overall shape now than I was then.

Well, I didn't think I was in very good shape.

I looked at my body which was thirty pounds leaner from the running, but was certainly not solid like when I had played defensive end at SMU. It was strange. I was still soft and I was still fat. I had come from 273 pounds and a body fat of 36% in September down to 240 pounds and 26% body fat. I thought about that. That's a lot of fat to lose and yet I couldn't believe how much further I needed to go. I had no muscle tone and was weak. Yes, I could run but that didn't take muscles or strength. Since I wasn't going to be a marathoner, I decided I needed a new physical challenge. I wanted something that involved lifting weights and muscle growth.

When I played football the workout stuff was hard but my body responded fast. As soon as I didn't have a coach barking at me, I slacked off. I hadn't lifted weights consistently in twenty-plus years and I didn't know what my body could do. I wanted to find out.

I had been a dues paying member of Lifetime Fitness for over a decade. I was their favorite type of club member. I paid, worked out maybe five times a year and otherwise left them alone. It was a waste but somehow I felt more fit just having a club membership.

Just like the marathon challenge, I needed to set a goal and then tell people about it. I decided to see if I could get into football playing shape again. The kind of shape I was in when I was twenty-one. I figured it would be no problem. After all, I was an athlete.

I gave myself thirty days of lifting weights to see if my body would respond and if I could summon the motivation to do it. Running had been relatively easy. I ran out the door and kept going until I was tired. I knew I was lucky and that I should have gotten hurt. But I didn't. Weight training would be different. At age 45 my muscles and joints had degraded like most middle aged guys, and since I had not regularly lifted since college I was destined to get hurt.

Then I thought that if I could get back in football playing shape, I might see if I could actually play football again. I did have two years of eligibility left. I thought if I could make the team I could prove to my daughter that I had done nothing wrong. Oddly, it made sense to me.

I told my wife I was going to get in football shape and try to play for SMU again. The marathon challenge was a test and I had passed it. This time, she decided to keep her doubts to herself. She couldn't be sure whether or not I might stick to the training. My plan involved lifting weights, sprinting, and dieting like a football player. It called for squats, dead lifts, power cleans, and all the other dangerous lifts that were sure to damage my back.

Kristin did suggest getting professionally trained; her biggest concern was that I might get seriously hurt. I told her I would be careful and hoped that she was wrong.

It was crazy thinking about getting into football shape and putting on pads again. But it was also motivating and exciting. I decided I needed a different story to tell people who might ask why I was lifting weights the way I was. I didn't mind people thinking I was crazy, I just didn't want to confirm it. The best story I could come up with was that I was training for *something*. I would leave it vague and trust that most people wouldn't care enough to press.

My fantasy of playing would be personal and told to only a few trusted people. But like most fantasies, the more I thought about it the more it seemed possible.

I imagined playing for SMU again, showing my kids that I could do it and cleaning up the past. As I got my mind wrapped around trying, I flashed back to my football career and how it ended. It wasn't like I never thought about playing again before, but it had always been a joke. Now I was sticking my toe in the water. Did I really have eligibility? Would SMU even embrace the idea?

As I headed to Lifetime Fitness for my first workout, I had not told anyone except my wife about my fantasy…I mean my workout goal. However in my mind, I was already in football shape. It was as good as done. I just needed to start lifting.

Chapter Nine:
1984-85 NCAA under Threat

We finished the 1984 season ranked #8 and looked forward to an even better 1985. We had lost a lot of players after the 1983 season but grew into a very good football team. As the only Southwest Conference team from the 1984 season to finish ranked, we were widely expected to win the conference again. Despite the NCAA rumblings, we were pre-season #3 and reporters wrote glowing stories of the success we were destined to achieve.

SMU reasonably hoped to sign a very strong recruiting class in 1985, but on the recruiting trail other schools had no problem talking up our ongoing NCAA investigation. That, combined with reporters asking about the investigation before asking about the team itself, made recruiting a challenge. As such, we signed an un-ranked but pretty good class. Considering all the background noise, it was a better class than we should have signed.

After signing day, Spring Football began and it was exciting. The weather in March was perfect. Mrs. Baird's Bread factory 100 yards away from campus at the corner of Mockingbird Lane and Central Expressway sent the aroma of freshly baked bread to us daily. Students emerged in shape for Spring Break beach vacations. All was right with the world. But behind the scenes the NCAA was working away on Sean Stopperich's allegations. He had gone to the NCAA in late October 1984 and the case should have been wrapped up by December. But the NCAA had more pressing problems.

1984 and 1985 were bad years for the NCAA and specifically for Executive Director Walter Byers. He spent the previous thirty-two years building up the power of the NCAA and it was now under mortal threat. His power rested on three things: the interpretation and enforcement of NCAA rules, revenue from college football television contracts, and more revenue from televising the NCAA March Madness basketball tournament.

During the early 1970's NCAA conventions, smaller schools had successfully placed limits on scholarships and recruiting. Those limits allowed schools that had been locked out of recruiting a shot at competing against the big boys. Not satisfied, the smaller schools began talk of a television revenue sharing plan the big schools derisively called "robin hood." The big schools were not interested in revenue sharing but didn't have the votes to prevent it, so they broke free and formed a new group called the College Football Association (CFA). The CFA was made up of most of the big time programs: all the members of the SWC (including SMU), SEC, Big Eight, ACC, WAC, and Notre Dame as well as other Independents. While still members of the NCAA these sixty-three schools started negotiating with the TV networks for their own contract in 1979.

Recognizing the threat, Byers lobbied hard to prevent the Big Ten and PAC Ten conferences from joining the new group. He still had loyal friends running those two conferences and they declined joining. In 1981 the CFA finalized their first television contract. Byers was incensed and promised to sanction any school that signed it. Most CFA members backed out of the contract in fear even though they won a court injunction preventing the NCAA from disciplining them.

The CFA responded to the threats by suing the NCAA for restraint of trade under the Sherman Anti-Trust Act. In 1983 the NCAA set aside an entire year's budget in anticipation of the US Supreme Court ruling against their monopoly. In 1984 the Court called the NCAA an illegal cartel. It ruled against them and invalidated all of their television contracts along with all of the revenue they received from the contracts. The financial loss represented over half of the entire NCAA budget. It was devastating. The NCAA was broke and at risk of sliding back down to their former status as a toothless scheduling organization.

Another threat appeared when three dozen university presidents thought it was time to get control of the NCAA and college athletics. The group proposed a Board of Presidents that would have veto power over NCAA convention actions. Their goal was to take away the power from the multitude of committees that worked within the NCAA operating structure.

The proposed Board was a direct threat to Byers' power source. So he worked behind the scenes to kill it and was ultimately successful by offering a watered down version. He proposed a President's Commission made up of the same Presidents but with different authority in its stead. The Commission would be empowered to meet once or twice a year and offer advice to the current NCAA committees. It was a fig leaf commission that placated a majority of schools and kept Byer's power structure largely in place.

Byers exercised a zero tolerance policy for rule breaking members but not when it came to himself. In 1985, the Washington Post reported that Byers arranged long term no-interest loans for himself and senior staff from the banks the NCAA used. He obtained lower than market interest rate loans from the United Missouri Bank of Kansas City, which was the NCAA's main bank. Then Byers offered to trade

NCAA land to a developer if he would extensively remodel his house for cost. The developer said Byers also worked out a similar arrangement with the architect who did design work for the NCAA's office buildings. The architect designed an addition for Byers' house for no cost. When Byers refused to honor the deals, the developer and architect sued. Court records showed Byers received the special treatment but the lawsuit was dropped when the architect died. People were outraged claiming the NCAA was a public institution. They demanded that those running the NCAA reveal what they knew about these shady deals. Byers argued he did nothing wrong.

The NCAA and Byers were getting hammered from everyone and everywhere. They were "too selective" in who they investigated, "college football had become too commercialized and they weren't doing enough to police it," and the NCAA was seen as nothing more than a "sports promoter masquerading as an educational enterprise." Jerry Tarkanian, Head Basketball Coach of UNLV, was grilling the NCAA in court over violations of his "due process" rights; that case was turning ugly. Facts about how the NCAA investigated schools, coaches, and players were spilling into the public arena revealing how the enforcement process was heavily and unfairly stacked in the NCAA's favor. The close relationship between the enforcement staff and Infractions Committee was being revealed; a pairing that allowed the NCAA to build their cases on hearsay alone and did not require them to share the bulk of their findings with targeted schools. With every day the NCAA breathed, it seemed things went from bad to worse. Byers and his staff must have wrung their hands. This was turning into a revolt. They were losing power.

Byers looked at his options and then did what he had always done when under threat: he attacked. He went public with a rare series of interviews and proclamations across the country. He was "very concerned" with all the cheating and that many universities were not helping to keep college sports clean. He was quoted as saying that "many athletes are getting as much as $20k in illegal payoffs, that his personal investigations showed that about 30% of schools cheat, that 60% were committing secondary violations and knew it, and the rest were committing secondary violations but were not aware." He commented on the threat to "amateurism" in college football that the CFA members represented, and that perhaps they should create an "open division." Maybe those schools "wanted to form their own semi-professional league." And since the NCAA was an advocate for strictly amateur sports, "those schools should just leave."

His comments shocked the sports world exactly as he had hoped.

By January 1985, at the annual NCAA convention in Nashville, executive director Walter Byers was more optimistic. Even though the NCAA's power had been slipping, he had skillfully assembled like-minded school presidents and promoted the idea that only the NCAA could "re-establish the direction of intercollegiate athletics and the spirit of integrity." He said, "We want to move toward a better day and commitment to the rules of intercollegiate athletics." These presidents wanted top down control of athletics programs and Byers was only too happy to help. They called for a Special Convention in June to specifically deal with cheating and to offer stiffer penalties for chronic violators.

At the Special Convention in New Orleans 793 college presidents met and voted on the harshest penalties against coaches and schools ever proposed: the so called "Death Penalty." The legislation was actually called the Repeat Violator Penalty and was designed to shut down an athletic program for two years if a school was found guilty of two major violations within a five-year period. The presidents were afraid that all the recent problems in college sports were tarnishing the good reputation of higher education and wanted a deterrent.

In voicing concerns about the broad based nature of the penalties and foreshadowing what was to come, SMU and other schools called into question the protection of due process rights for individuals and institutions. Others were concerned that innocent people would be punished with such a broad brushed penalty. While still more were concerned that top football programs could bounce right back from such a penalty while mid-level programs might never make it back.

Frank Remington, Chairman of the NCAA Infractions Committee, said that "before the NCAA could decide to ban a program, it would also have to consider several other factors. You aren't just hurting the schools, there is the conference, and the teams it was supposed to play. It's a concern to not harm those who have done nothing wrong." Strangely, I never heard those sentiments again.

The vote to institute the Death Penalty carried 427 to 6. Half of the "no" votes came from a strange alliance of SMU, Texas, and Texas A&M. The alliance made no sense other than as a last minute understanding that their backstabbing had brought about these new NCAA powers.

On September 1, 1985 any repeat major infraction that occurred within a five-year period would be eligible for the penalty. But some schools would be at significantly more risk. Just before the rule was adopted it was modified to include a look back period. That meant any violation within the last five years would count against a school's record as a first strike. For those schools it would only take one strike to trigger death.

It worked. The NCAA and Walter Byers had successfully deflected the attention from their own ethical problems and the failings of the NCAA itself to the more broad failings of institutional cheating within the college ranks. With those moves their power was renewed as the only force powerful enough to clean up college football. Now, they needed to demonstrate that power.

Chapter Ten:
1985 - Sean Stopperich and the Boosters

After Stopperich withdrew from SMU and began talking to the NCAA, SMU's leaders knew they had a problem. Our strategy had been to fight the NCAA every step of the way. We argued that we were selectively investigated and that we were doing nothing different from most of our conference rivals, not to mention what other top programs around the country were doing. The hypocrisy of our conference rivals that had turned us in was rich, and we felt no obligation to help the NCAA in their pursuit of us.

Now things were different. Stopperich was a player from inside SMU's walls who was paid, turned, and knew the specifics. SMU had to change its strategy.

I was paying attention to the NCAA investigation and reading all I could get my hands on. When I came to SMU in 1984 there was an ongoing investigation. But since many schools were being looked at by the NCAA for all sorts of things, I wasn't too concerned. I knew that the investigation was the result of an intense 1983 SWC recruiting season; a recruiting contest that SMU won by signing the #6 class in the country. Our reward came three weeks later in the form of a Preliminary Letter of Inquiry from the NCAA to SMU President L. Donald Shields on March 10, 1983. That confidential letter was sent per the NCAA Rules of Procedure and signified the opening of an NCAA investigation.

Initially there were allegations of cars, cash and summer jobs being offered to recruits that signed with our rivals in the Southwest Conference. Most of the allegations were made by current University of Texas players but there were a few from Texas A&M and even a Texas kid that had signed with Iowa. A handful of SMU kids were named but they were players Texas recruited, lost, and then put on the NCAA list. The Texas players were solicited by Coach Fred Akers at the behest of Athletic Director Deloss Dodds.

Texas was in a drought. They had been the dominant force within the conference for years but had fallen. They were losing top recruits to SMU and even Houston and TCU. Deloss Dodds worked previously with Executive Director Byers on the NCAA Rules Committee and was considered an expert in NCAA rules. His long standing personal relationship with Byers gave him a direct pipeline to feed his allegations. But the problem with using UT's recruits to target SMU was that they only had allegations of offers *made* and not of offers *accepted.* The NCAA needed proof from somebody who had been offered, accepted the offer, and then gone to SMU.

After two years of searching and looking for anything that would stick, the NCAA's witch hunt was finally reduced to a surprise SMU witness: Sean Stopperich. He told the NCAA that a booster had given him $5,000 and promised more money to cover monthly expenses. The total allegedly paid to Stopperich and his family was $11,000. He never said any coach or any member of the school did anything other than one coach gave his sister a keychain. According to Stopperich, "I really don't think that Head Coach Bobby Collins knows what's going on, but maybe he doesn't want to know."

In April 1985 we had a pretty good idea of all of the charges. They were recruiting violations over the previous two years by our "unaffiliated representatives" or boosters as they were called. At the time and for decades before it was normal for boosters to be around their college teams. They hung out in the locker rooms, flew on team planes, and interacted with players. It happened at SMU and I know it happened elsewhere.

Not only did the boosters hang out with the players, they hung out with the coaches. They became friends. They became compatriots in the pursuit of winning teams. A coach might mention a kid's name or suggest that a booster from a recruit's home town could help out with recruiting. These same boosters then knew which high school players were high on the list for their alma maters. In this way boosters were invited to help and enjoyed doing so.

Our boosters were not out there recruiting alone. It was crowded. Coaches and boosters from numerous colleges, politicians (LBJ had UT recruits flown out to his ranch), high school coaches on the take, and even paid scouts helped point recruits towards *their* preferred schools. At SMU there was no policy of paying players a certain amount of money or giving them a car. The policy was simply a strategy to help sign a recruit.

On the other side, in most cases the recruits that were being fought over were poor like Stopperich and football represented a way out. It took two to tango and recruits had no problem telling other schools what they had been offered as a way of promoting a bid system for their talents. It was a perfect match. Wealthy boosters from various schools fought over poor kids to commit to their college and the recruits played the system for all it was worth.

The state of Texas was probably the worst due to the high number of great recruits in the state and the fact that eight of the nine SWC schools were located here. Other schools like Oklahoma thought Texas was their recruiting territory too. We were tripping over each other. Most of the time the money flowing was pocket change; $20 or $100 for entertainment or meals, maybe tickets to a game. The boosters felt no guilt and the schools did not try to rein them in.

At SMU, our boosters were school supporters and football fans. They were wealthy but by no means were they the wealthiest supporters of the school. The wealthiest boosters would not have gotten dirty in a south Dallas or inner city Houston high school. Most of them shared the common background of having been self-made men. They knew what it was like to play football and have no money for a date or gas. They had been there. When they were invited to help recruit, they happily did so. But it needs to be emphasized, they were *invited* to help. They were not out there throwing money at recruits of their own volition.

We were involved in a type of cold war. Texas and Texas A&M as the big state schools felt that they owned the state. Upstart University of Houston had been mining the inner city Houston schools for years and achieved success in blocking the big boys out. SMU and TCU decided to get serious in the recruiting game and aggressively pursued players that the big boys thought they had locked up. Boosters were leveling the playing field in recruiting. No longer could the big state schools sit back and expect the best players. They would have to fight for them.

Once Stopperich went public we could either support our boosters who had been helping the coaches recruit, or we could sell them out in hopes of NCAA leniency. SMU chose to say that we had nothing to do with the boosters' actions. We preemptively tried to reduce our penalties by blaming all of the violations on nine boosters that were "out of control." We said they were illicitly involved in recruiting players to SMU secretly and that they did it alone.

SMU would not name them for legal reasons but most of the boosters were easily identifiable. Then SMU disassociated several of them from the university's athletic programs as a way of initiating "corrective actions." Before the verdict, the NCAA asked whether SMU funds or funds from any other source were being paid to student athletes in violation of NCAA rules. SMU's written response was a denial that SMU funds were ever used for such purposes. The response made no reference to funds from other sources.

The NCAA accepted that the boosters were solely to blame for all the recruiting irregularities, and then they hit SMU with the hardest set of penalties they had ever handed down. Not only was there no mercy, they specifically cited the interaction of the boosters as why they handed down the crippling penalties.

Chapter Eleven:
1985 Penalty - Strike One

The NCAA issued their initial infractions report May 1985 and the penalties were devastating. Tired of chasing us for two years, the NCAA decided to drop the hammer. There had been many twists and turns in the twenty-nine month investigation. The alleged cars, cash, and summer jobs were not included in the NCAA report as violations. Numerous athletes at SMU and other schools who supposedly had been offered illicit things were interviewed to no avail. All the allegations from Texas players were included in the infractions report but there was nothing really to those. Stopperich was the game changer. He was the player the NCAA had been looking and hoping for and we had no defense against him. They knew that they had not uncovered everything but he was enough.

We appealed the penalties to the NCAA Appeals Committee and lost as every other school before and after us have lost. According to the NCAA enforcement staff, "Universities always lose and should always lose." Why they have an appeals committee, I don't know. I suppose it's to make the member schools feel like they have some due process rights. But really, why bother if nobody ever wins an appeal?

It was necessary to exhaust all of our NCAA options if we were going to sue the NCAA for selective enforcement like we had been threatening. They bet that we would not challenge them in court and risk future interviews under oath. The NCAA was right. We did not risk a trial and the potentially more harmful revelations that might come out. With no other options, on August 16, 1985 we accepted the NCAA verdict.

Citing Southern Methodist University's "history of involvement" in rules violations we were hit with: three years of probation through August 1988, two years of postseason bowl bans (1985 and 1986 Seasons), no live television in 1986, the complete loss of all thirty scholarships in the 1986 recruiting class, and the reduction to a maximum of fifteen scholarships in the 1987 recruiting class (net reduction of forty-five scholarships). The NCAA also imposed a first ever total banishment of boosters from recruiting during the probationary period. By not using outside representatives (boosters) for three years, the NCAA and SMU hoped to "gain a more balanced perspective among supporters of the football program."

The infractions themselves were relatively minor: one paid player (Stopperich), money from a booster with no direct tie in to SMU or the coaching staff, and allegations of offers from boosters to players who went to our rival schools. The Infractions Committee had the discretion to impose serious penalties if a school demonstrated an ongoing pattern of violations. It was this discretion and not the actual violations that they used to justify their penalties. They had uncovered no structural payment system and no proof of official SMU involvement. Nothing hinted at involvement by Head Coach Bobby Collins. Staff members were only circumstantially linked.

The penalty was in line with a new resolution adopted that year by the American Football Coaches Association urging the NCAA to make greater use of scholarship cuts in punishing rule-breakers. Previously, the NCAA only had three penalties: TV bans, postseason bans, and the "stigma" of probation. The NCAA needed to find a new penalty in 1984 when it lost control of the TV contracts. It hit upon scholarship reductions and by doing so significantly raised the cost of cheating. Never before or since has the NCAA forced a school to, in effect forfeit an entire recruiting class.

The penalties were devastating not just because they would prevent us from attaining a national championship in 1985 or 1986, but because the reduction in scholarships could knock us from national prominence and render us uncompetitive for years. The NCAA wanted to make an example of SMU with the forty-five scholarship reduction. It was the closest thing to a two-year Death Penalty they had without that specific penalty in effect. Gradually, it was expected the penalty would cut our team in half. Then it would take even more time to build back to full strength.

The practical effect of those cuts would be a slow and drawn out death as our roster dwindled downward. With this penalty the NCAA was sure they had knocked us out and also sent a strong message to the membership. They were in charge. They had the power to destroy a program and they were willing to use it.

We players had been speculating. The investigation and then the penalties were daily fixtures in the newspapers. We knew something was coming and now we knew what it was. We had expected bad but not that bad, and nobody knew how we would react. This was supposed to be our year. We were chosen to make a run at the national championship. The September 14 SMU vs. Oklahoma game had even been moved to December 7 for an end of season showdown between two hopefully top ranked teams.

The investigation and the infractions occurred before the September 1 trigger date for the Death Penalty so we dodged the penalty this time. But it counted as our first strike.

For the next five years any new major infraction would trigger death. One more strike and we were done.

I thought of Sean and what would have happened if he hadn't gone to SMU. The 1983-85 NCAA witch hunt would have been a bust. He was a nice enough kid and I think he and I were a lot alike. Pennsylvania and Colorado football were both good, but they weren't like Texas football. A lot of us came to SMU thinking we were great football players. Then we all learned how much more competitive and hard it was here. Football was a religion in Texas; it had been a sport in Colorado. I struggled being so far from home. I hated not being better than average on the field. A lot of us, including Sean, struggled. But Sean took things too personally. He would have played at SMU if he stayed, but he didn't have the dedication to stay with it.

The NCAA offered Sean immunity for his testimony and evidence against SMU. They also allowed him to transfer and play football again even though he solicited and accepted the booster money. Both parties were guilty but only SMU had to pay. I have no doubt that if SMU could go back in time we would have released Sean from his Letter of Intent. He could have gone back to Pittsburgh happy and SMU could have continued being a football powerhouse. Instead SMU played poker with a guy who had nothing to lose, and we lost.

Sean wasn't the big winner though. He enrolled back home at Pitt and worked out there for a year, but Pitt never offered him a scholarship. Across the state and a step down, Temple University was interested. They offered Sean a scholarship which he accepted. He enrolled at Temple, sat out the 1985 season and made the team in 1986. He never really played there or found the success he craved. He didn't make the pros and ended up part owner of a gym.

David Richards told me that he ran in to Sean in Pittsburgh in 1995 at a bar frequented by former college and professional players. They had some heated words about what Sean did to SMU and it got physical. He tried to argue that he wasn't responsible for the resulting Death Penalty but David wasn't buying it. They had been best friends. For Richards, the betrayal was bigger than SMU. When the bar owners found out Sean was the player that had turned in SMU he was banned from the bar. I'm sure Sean had spent numerous years explaining that it wasn't his fault to whoever would listen. Unfortunately, the argument ended a few weeks later when Sean died of a drug overdose.

Chapter Twelve:
2011 - Getting in Shape

Before I hit the weights at Lifetime Fitness I wanted to recheck my fantasy. After all, twenty-five years is a long time. I kept thinking about playing again and couldn't get it out of my head. I decided I needed to bounce the idea off of someone who was close to SMU athletics.

The person I chose was Mike Shore. Mike was a fraternity brother and roommate from college. He was now a successful attorney with his own big time law firm. He was also a huge SMU athletics supporter. When SMU decided to get serious about rebuilding the football program in 2007, they raised money from select alumni to hire a top tier football coach. Mike was one of the twenty members of the "Circle of Champions" that each contributed $500,000 to the cause and Coach June Jones was the hire.

As such, Mike had a pipeline into the athletic department and their plans. I told him I had a crazy idea for something and wanted his counsel. He agreed to meet with me and we set a date. The day before our meeting I called and told him some specifics of my idea so he could digest it beforehand. I wanted him to have time to sufficiently consider my project and maybe present it to some of his SMU connections.

We met on Wednesday January 19, 2011 at Snuffer's restaurant on lower Greenville Avenue, a Dallas and SMU institution. Mike told me he called SMU Athletic Director Steve Orsini the night before and explained my plan to him. According to Mike, Steve expressed surprise and interest that there was a guy from the 1980's team that didn't transfer, still had eligibility, and wanted to play again. Mike told me they were open to it and I was pleased. He told me he thought I should go for it and gave me Orsini's cell number to discuss it with him further. It was still just a crazy idea but maybe, just maybe, SMU would support me on this quest.

I began to hit the weights. My wife was nervous I would get hurt and pressed me to get a personal trainer. I told myself I knew what I was doing because I was an athlete. But it had been a long time and I really didn't know. Weight training had changed radically over the last twenty-five years. In my day, we used to load up the barbells and get after it. We hurt ourselves a lot, concentrated on show exercises, and became too strong in lifts that were not important for playing football. We squatted, bench pressed, dead lifted, and clean and jerked really heavy weight. Now apparently there is this thing called "core" and athletes strive for explosiveness over strength. They no longer try to lift a maximum weight; they lift lighter weight with more repetitions.

Maybe Kristin was right. Maybe I did need a trainer. Quietly I asked around the club and identified a couple of trainers that had been athletes and looked like they knew what they were doing. I lined them up as possible trainers if I decided I needed them. But first, I wanted to see what I could do.

The first thing a guy does in a gym is bench press. I don't know why. It was that way in the 1980's and apparently it's still true today. The bench press is pretty worthless as a fitness tool but you can put a lot of weight on a bar and then lay down. It's perfect...unless you haven't done it for a while. The first week after lifting, I felt like every muscle in my body was torn and on fire. Everything seized up and hurt. My back throbbed and stabbed at me like it was bone-on-bone. My groin locked up. I needed help getting off the toilet. I walked like I was an eighty year old man.

I kept after it though and by the second and third weeks I started to feel better. I wasn't as strong as in my football days but I could tell there was such a thing as muscle memory.

By mid-February I had been lifting for about a month and started to believe that I could get strong enough to play. My goals were to get close to the NFL Combine standards in size, strength, and speed for defensive ends. I wanted to lose another 11% body fat to get down to 15%. I wanted to gain weight back up to at least 265 pounds. I wanted to bench press 225 pounds twenty-five times, run a 4.8 or better 40-yard dash, and squat 315 pounds fifteen times. I figured with those numbers I wouldn't get killed by the current college players.

I started needing spotters. To get a decent spotter I would ask a guy who looked the most like he knew what he was doing. That was not a guarantee of a good spot. Some guys lift it off you so you don't even struggle with it and some guys make you struggle too much. Neither of these types of spots is helpful or safe. That was yet another reason for me to get a trainer.

One of the spotters I used was a guy named Scott. He was shorter than me, a little stockier and had obviously been an athlete. He played college football as a fullback until a series of concussions and a knee injury took him out. Then he played semi-professional softball. Currently, he was a private athletic trainer who just happened to also workout at Lifetime Fitness. He gave great spots. One day, it was bench day and I was going for twelve repetitions of 225. I struggled and didn't get it. Scott said, "I don't want to stick my nose in your business, but what are you trying to do?"

What he meant was: Why was a forty-five-year-old guy in poor condition struggling with that much weight when all that was going to happen would be getting hurt?

I can't prove it, but I think my wife put him up to it.

I had already decided not to tell that many people about my quest until it was more of a reality. But here was a guy I didn't know who could serve as a sounding board for my crazy idea. I told Scott that I played football for SMU in the 1980's during the Death Penalty years and because of the penalty I had two years of eligibility remaining. I told him I intended to use them. He laughed and asked if I was serious.

Then he said, "Holy crap...you can do it."

"Yes," I told him. "Yes, I can."

I asked Scott if he didn't have any injuries and could go back and play one more season, would he do it? That is a question any former athlete has to consider. If you had the chance, would you try?

The next day Scott came up to me and said, "I want to help you do it." He said he couldn't sleep and kept revisiting the question of whether he would play again if he could. He was excited about the idea of helping me make it happen. He didn't work for Lifetime so he couldn't accept any pay and we agreed to just meet and workout. Together, we began the journey over the next seven months to get me in shape to play college football again.

We worked out six days a week for two plus hours a day. It was fierce. I quickly learned that I really didn't know what I was doing and that I needed to build up core and secondary muscles in addition to my main strength muscles. If I didn't do that, I would get hurt. We used bands and incorporated resistance training into our routine. He counseled me to eat a lot. He said the way I was working out it would be a struggle to eat enough. I started drinking protein shakes and eating 5 times a day. I slowly gained weight and lost fat. I was getting stronger. Incredibly it was working.

One day I decided to go to the SMU campus and buy an SMU workout shirt. I hadn't owned an SMU shirt since I was in college. Somehow, working out to play football at SMU again made it all right. I was a bit embarrassed to wear the shirt to the gym. After twenty-five years of refusing to speak about SMU football now I was wearing an SMU football shirt. Proudly displaying the Pony, I decided to continue wearing the shirt once or twice a week at the gym until I became completely comfortable with the concept of being an SMU football supporter. Then I bought another shirt.

Strangely, it felt good. I was getting bigger and starting to look like a football player again. People in the gym began asking me what I was training for. Others asked if I had played football for SMU. Still others asked if I was a coach at SMU. I didn't mind. In the gym there were all kinds of people wearing their college shirts. I saw shirts supporting Texas, Texas A&M, LSU, Oregon, and even Colorado State. But there were very few SMU shirts. I get it. I knew there were lots of SMU alums in the gym but not many of us were proudly showing it.

I was beginning to re-engage with my university and it felt right. SMU pride was slowly creeping back into my blood. I started to believe I could physically do it and would be able to play. I wondered how much further this adventure might really go.

Chapter Thirteen:
1985 Season

The first football game of our 1985 season was one week away. We were playing UTEP on September 7 and officially my redshirt season would be over. This was my sophomore year and I was the number five defensive end rotating between the left and right side as needed. Technically I would be called a redshirt freshman because it was my first year playing in games. Regardless of what I was called, I couldn't wait to get on the field and start knocking guys around. Looming over my enthusiasm, the long shadow cast on our team from the recent NCAA penalties was disrupting.

In late August after the penalties were announced, the coaches walked us through the ramifications of our situation. We players could have gotten dejected and given up. Instead we had a team meeting without the coaches and discussed our options. All of us had come to SMU when it was the winningest program in the country and we would now finish our careers on probation without bowl eligibility. The leaders of our team, guys like running back Reggie Dupard and nose tackle Jerry Ball pushed us to stay together and play for each other. We talked about how we were a team that had been under constant pressure from the media and NCAA. We talked about how we were not quitters.

We discussed the fact that we had options. Per NCAA guidelines upperclassmen could transfer away without having to sit out a year to play for other schools free of probation and with better media coverage. Underclassmen would have to sit out a year if we transferred, but we could escape the sanctions. We had all been sure we would be playing for a national championship this season. Now we would be playing only for pride. It was discouraging but not one of our players transferred. We all decided to stay at SMU and play as a team, no matter the outcome.

On the outside we projected a confident attitude. Practices were great and we looked forward to winning, possibly going undefeated and being #1 even with the NCAA restrictions. It was possible. Normally you have to play in a bowl to be worthy of a national championship but if we went 11-0 in the regular season and finished well against Oklahoma we believed that our record would weigh heavily in the voting. With no BCS or playoff system in place, we had a shot. On the inside we worried about the challenges we faced. One thing we all agreed on was that our probation would be no excuse for playing poorly

For the 1985 season we planned on more of what made SMU great in the early 1980's: an option based tailback system rotating in two different tailbacks behind two rotating offensive lines. The system was designed to maintain ball control and intensity for four full quarters. Our two offensive lines averaged 6'- 3" and 285 pounds, larger than the Dallas Cowboys and most NFL lines of the era. The rotating line theory began at SMU in 1982 under line coach and offensive coordinator Whitey Jordan. With this strategy we would be fresh in the fourth quarter and expected to grind down and score against a more tired opponent. We balanced both lines so that one line was not overly dominant vs. the other. Each game we gave both tailbacks and offensive lines a fairly equal number of snaps. We rarely lost a game in the fourth quarter.

We opened a little slow at home against UTEP on September 7. We won 35-23 but had to rally in the fourth quarter. UTEP was actually leading 17-14 in the third quarter when we put it in gear and scored three touchdowns. We moved the ball well and had 522 yards of offense but we were still working out the kinks and were not consistent.

Our next game against TCU was a long three weeks later on September 28. This was due to the rescheduled Oklahoma game. During our layoff we had time to work out those kinks. At TCU our offense kicked in and we showed what we could do. We won 56 – 21 and set a school record with total offense of 636 yards before a national TV audience on ESPN. At the half we were winning 35-7 and then throttled down in the second. Running backs Reggie Dupard (182 yards) and Jeff Atkins (139 yards) scored three touchdowns each with every drive over fifty-five yards. Two additional throwing touchdowns by quarterbacks Don King and Bobby Watters finished off the scoring. On the defensive side, our linemen shut down their inside running and our linebackers completely closed off the outside game. TCU never really had a chance.

We were 2 - 0 and cruising on October 5 when we traveled to Tucson to play the University of Arizona Wildcats. We were ranked #3 in the country behind Iowa and Oklahoma. Before the game we led the nation in total offense and were second in rushing, third in scoring. As we prepared to take the field we heard Iowa was losing to Michigan State. All we had to do was beat unranked Arizona to move to #2. Iowa would ultimately rally and beat Michigan State late in that game but we didn't know that. Our eyes focused on our "bowl" game against Oklahoma.

Arizona wasn't a real challenge to our plan; they were merely in the way. As we ran onto the field, Arizona fans threw monopoly money at us and yelled all kinds of "paid player" insults. This was new. They were louder and ruder than anything we ever experienced in Texas or from our conference rivals. Throughout the game their fans never stopped the taunts. It had an impact.

Arizona saw themselves as giant killers and they were. They took advantage of our mistakes and shocked us in the second quarter with three touchdown passes during an eleven minute span. Two of their scores came off SMU fumbles and two interceptions in the fourth quarter prevented our comeback. It didn't matter. Our offense couldn't move the ball and they beat us 28-6. We needed to win that game. We certainly shouldn't have played poorly because of their loud fans or because we overlooked an average team, but we did. That night our season took a huge hit as we realized our end of season dream to play Oklahoma for the national championship was over. Monday after the Arizona loss we dropped to #16.

Next up was #19 Baylor. They were building up their program and saw us as in their way. They took an early two-touchdown lead in the second quarter until we were able to tie the game at halftime. In the second half, Baylor's defense rallied as we fumbled on their two-yard line and they got key sacks to stop our drives. They put together one last drive to take the lead 21-14 and the win.

That loss dropped us from the rankings and threatened to derail our chances for even a winning season. We traveled to Houston to face a rebuilding team that had beaten us last year and cost us a Cotton Bowl invite. Reggie Dupard (184 yards and 2 touchdowns) and Jeff Atkins (112 yards and 1 touchdown) saddled up and ran like the Pony Express of old. We ran only nine different offensive plays that included basic inside runs and outside options. Combined with play-action passes we never had to make any changes or throw the ball much. Our alternating lines wore them down. The final score was 37-13. We were feeling good again. Next up was #19 Texas.

SMU and Texas had been beating on each other for years. We had great talent and coaching but so did they. The rivalry between us was getting more heated. In the past we cost each other both conference and national championships. We beat them in 1980 and 82. They were our only losses in 1981 and 83. We won the conference in 1981, 82, and 84 while they won it in 1983 and expected to again this year.

They thought we were a snobby rich school and we thought them a lowly community college. Texas had been the main source behind the referrals to the NCAA about us and was thus indirectly responsible for our recent probation.

With this as history, the Longhorns came to Texas Stadium on October 26 having only lost a close game to #2 Oklahoma. The 1985 Texas vs. SMU game in Dallas was about more than bragging rights, it was personal. We hated each other.

Before the game, Texas' coach Fred Akers said that the SMU game shouldn't count in the Southwest Conference standings since we were on probation. He was right to worry about that because we were gunning for them. As the game began it was obvious that SMU was going to win. We moved the ball. We got all the breaks, be it SMU fumbles that turned into SMU touchdowns or Texas fumbles that turned into SMU recoveries.

The key play of the game started from our five yard line. Fullback Cobby Morrison broke free and was bolting down the sideline for the end zone. Texas safety Tony Tillmon caught him at the UT 30 and caused Morrison to fumble. As the ball tumbled on the field a trailing receiver, Jeffrey Jacobs, caught the loose ball in midair and ran the remaining thirty yards without breaking stride for the score. Four fumbles, two interceptions, and that one play all but deflated and overwhelmed a hapless Texas team. The final score was Southern Methodist 44 and the University of Texas 14. It wasn't even that close and it could have been worse. We took it easy on them in the fourth quarter and played our reserves.

It was an old fashioned Texas ass-kicking the likes of which Texas hadn't seen in years and they knew it. It was the worst whipping SMU had ever given to Texas. It was an embarrassing loss and SMU had big bragging rights.

Coming off a powerhouse win like that we had to travel to Texas A&M for another big challenge. We were ranked again (#20) and A&M was a better team than their 4-2 record. Kyle Field had 55k passionate Aggies and cadets with unsheathed swords who stood and chanted the entire time. They knew that the SMU game was make or break for their season.

The first half was all defense and mistakes. SMU scored first when Dupard ran it in late in the 1st quarter followed by an A&M field goal. A&M then returned the 2nd half kickoff 71 yards to set up the go ahead score, 10-7. A&M blocked a tying 20 yard field goal and more penalties and mistakes on both sides prevented any scores until SMU kicker Brandy Brownlee kicked a 33 yard field goal to tie the game with 10:22 left. The Aggies answered and drove the length of the field to score and then missed the PAT. Two minutes later SMU drove 91 yards to score and hit the PAT for a 17-16 lead. But A&M was able to get close enough for a 48 yard field goal to win 19-17 as the game ended.

For our team the rest of the season was a struggle. We soldiered on and rallied to win our next two games. But then we dropped another tough one to Arkansas 15-9. We had gotten to the end of the season and we were not where we planned to be. We were 6 – 4 and unranked heading up to Norman, Oklahoma and our supposed "bowl" game. Meanwhile, Oklahoma had done what they set out to do. They were 10 – 1 and ranked #3. They were playing for the national championship while we were trying to salvage the worst season any of us had ever experienced.

It was no contest. The final was 35 -13 and they beat us that day on both sides of the ball. They were truly a great team and proved it again a month later in the Orange Bowl by beating Penn State to become the 1985 National Champions.

We finished 6 - 5 but we were a better team than our record indicated. We lost the main driver for our season when

Arizona beat us. Mentally we never recovered and we played the rest of the season erratically. Yes, we got up for Texas but then we lost close ones to Baylor, Texas A&M, and Arkansas.

The NCAA, the bite of the sanctions, hostile crowds and media, and other distractions were just too much. The season we dreamed of, became just that, a dream.

Chapter Fourteen:
1986 - Storm Clouds

My second season as a Mustang had been a disappointment. We had a winning season and we would have been bowl eligible if we weren't on probation. But the five losses in one season equaled the total number of games SMU lost in the previous three seasons combined. The Pony Express was wobbling.

Then came February 1986 and National Signing Day. The NCAA sanctions of August 1985 were starting to hurt in real terms. We had no scholarships to offer recruits. We watched helplessly as we lost great players to our rivals and we knew what that meant for the future.

Somehow SMU convinced around fifteen scholarship level players to walk on to our program. We needed them. They had no guarantee that a scholarship would ever be available. But they had the opportunity to make the roster of a top twenty team and the rest was up to them. As our numbers dwindled we would become more dependent on players like these growing into players that could help.

By the time spring ball rolled around, SMU was in need of some positive press. We held our allowable twenty days of practices but hanging over our heads was always that nasty probation. There would be no live television and no postseason games in the 1986 season and then fifteen more scholarship cuts to look forward to in 1987. The deteriorating situation was constantly on our minds.

The decision was made to change the annual Spring Red – Blue game between a divided SMU squad into a game between the current SMU team and an "older" team made up of ex-gridiron greats. Eric Dickerson, Wes Hopkins, Russell Carter, and Michael Carter from recent days, and many others from more distant days were all scheduled to suit up and play. The alumni were coached by former SMU and NFL legends Forrest Gregg of the Green Bay Packers and Raymond Berry of the New England Patriots. The game wasn't really close but that wasn't the point. We needed some positive things to talk about. Even though the two-year negative drumbeat of the NCAA investigation was finally over, the pain of its sanctions was continuing. With the Spring Red-Blue game, at least for one day we could relive the greatness of SMU football and remember who we were.

As spring ended, many considered the SWC the best conference in the country. SMU was on probation but still had a lot of talent. A&M was ranked top five, Baylor and Arkansas top fifteen, and Texas had a shot at top twenty due to their consistently high recruiting classes. Only Arkansas had lost significant starters from the previous year.

Overshadowing the SWC's potential was the NCAA. Almost the entire conference was under investigation. TCU was waiting for their sanctions. Texas, Texas A&M, Houston, and Texas Tech all had NCAA investigators on campus. Only Rice, Baylor, and Arkansas would survive that year without sanctions for major violations. Nobody really knew how all the NCAA distractions would affect those schools and the SWC race. At least for us we knew, our investigation was old news.

Across town TCU was dealing with the results of their NCAA troubles. Coach Wacker had been very vocal about running a clean program. He was so vocal that the month after we were hammered by the NCAA in 1985, seven of his best players decided to come forward to tell him they had accepted thousands of dollars in payments from their boosters. Coach Wacker immediately suspended all seven players and turned in his program. TCU hoped that the NCAA would be lenient due to the self-reporting policy the NCAA was promoting. Wacker eventually went so far as to tell the NCAA that as many as twenty-nine current and former players had accepted improper payments. That kind of candidness was unheard of.

In May 1986 Coach Wacker discovered the cold, hard reality that the self-reporting promotion of the NCAA was a crock. David Berst and the NCAA in a showing of no sympathy, *whacked* TCU with three-years' probation, suspended the guilty players, banned them from a 1986 bowl, made them forfeit all TV revenue from the 1983 and 1984 seasons, and eliminated thirty-five scholarships over two years. The NCAA cited sixty-four violations of NCAA bylaws, saying the TCU case was one of the worst it had ever investigated.

While the infractions were serious, every single violation was self-reported. The NCAA discovered nothing that TCU hadn't handed them. It was stunning. Wacker himself was clearly trying to run a clean program and TCU did everything the NCAA could have hoped a program would do in self-reporting. The result? No leniency. None.

Wacker was livid when he found out their punishment, especially since most of the violations occurred under TCU's previous coach. Speaking to the media he called it "the living death penalty" and said, "I think we just set back self-disclosure." Wacker could have quietly shut the payments down and continued rebuilding the Frog program. Instead he followed the letter of law and was punished severely for his honesty. No program would make that mistake again.

Around the country something else was happening. It became cool to turn in your alma mater. Two dozen former Kentucky basketball players turned in their own program for giving them money. Charles Barkley turned in Auburn and Terry Catledge turned in South Alabama for do-nothing jobs and substantial cash payments. Even former University of Texas players went public with ticket selling and cash handshake stories. The media jumped on the bandwagon breaking stories at numerous universities around the country. However, media stories were not enough to prove violations. These players and unnamed sources would have to repeat their stories to NCAA investigators for the evidence to be used. In follow-up stories and NCAA interviews, players quickly recanted or altered their statements and usually that was the end of the investigation.

The NCAA was not immune to all the publicly disclosed violations. They did not need major stories of cheating dissolving into dismissed charges or dropped cases. Therefore it was important for the NCAA to reach a player *before* he recanted. Because they responded quickly to some and slowly to others, the NCAA soon became widely perceived as selective in their enforcement and soft on the major sports programs.

After all, if they didn't want to nail a program they could take their time interviewing witnesses. And if they did want to nail a program, they could speed it up.

Chapter Fifteen:
1986 Season

By the time the 1986 football season rolled around I was tired of thinking about all the NCAA crap going on around the country and in the SWC. We had one more year of sanctions and then we were done. For the 1987 season we would be allowed to be on live television and eligible for postseason play. The scholarship restrictions would be over. It was encouraging to me and for all of us younger players. We just had to hang tough. We were almost there.

With a stubborn attitude our team was determined to make the most of a tough situation. Yes, we were on probation. Yes, our roster had been reduced to seventy-one scholarship players and fifteen freshman walk-ons. Yes, we were under a TV and Bowl ban.

But we had survived this far. We decided to stay and play at SMU. We were not going to quit. Picked as one of the best teams in the country pre-season 1985, now we were picked to finish sixth or seventh in the conference. Those rankings didn't mean much before a season began and we planned to prove them wrong.

We went into the season relatively problem free. Other schools were just starting to implement NCAA drug testing while SMU had already dealt with it and only lost a few players. Our biggest problem was a tough schedule that included: Arizona State, Baylor, Texas, and Notre Dame on the road. And Boston College, TCU, Texas A&M, and Arkansas at home. A six or seven win season would have been considered a success by a full strength team much less a team like ours playing twenty-five short.

Position by position we still matched up pretty well. But because of the reduced roster, our depth at key positions was already gone. Changes were necessary. According to Offensive Coordinator Whitey Jordan, "Your personnel dictates your offense." Coaches Collins and Jordan flew out to San Diego to study a new passing offense with the San Diego Chargers. "Air Coryell" it was called after legendary NFL coach Don Coryell. They came back and created a completely new team.

Since the days of the Pony Express with Eric Dickerson and Craig James through the Reggie Dupard and Jeff Atkins days, SMU ran a tandem running back scheme and contended for national championships. Not this year. Not anymore. We were too thin at offensive line and in the backfield to continue with a tandem back offense. It would be just Jeff Atkins as a single back. He was a great running back but it was a big change.

In addition to the change in running, the plan was to open up the passing game. Quarterback Bobby Watters was more of a passing quarterback in high school but at SMU had rarely thrown the ball. The new scheme called for passing on first down, passing to backs in the flat, short passes for ball control, and of course running the ball. It may sound like fundamental football today, but for us this was a radical departure from the previous six-year reliance on double tailbacks and rotating lines.

On the defensive side we changed the line from a 5-2 scheme to a 4-3 to avoid easy double teams. The change revolved around Jerry Ball who was all-conference as nose guard being moved to left tackle with Terence Mann on the right. We didn't have depth at linebacker, but our starters were solid. Our secondary was probably better than before with strong returners and very talented younger players.

While we suffered no illusions of a national title, we thought we could play and thought we had a chance to be great. We couldn't afford any injuries and we would have to have players step up and come through, but that was nothing new for this team.

We opened September 13 at Rice who we beat the previous nine years straight. Our new offense started slow. Watters bounced his first pass five yards in front of the receiver and fumbled away on the first two possessions. But then we started clicking. Watters passed for 236 yards and two touchdowns and ran for another. Jeff Atkins had 86 yards rushing and Ron Morris had six catches for 123 yards and a touchdown...all in the first half. Rice never recovered once our offense settled in, and by the time it was over we had 513 yards of total offense and had won 45-3.

September 20 we traveled to #18 Arizona State and got soundly beaten 30-0. It was our first shutout since 1980. The score wasn't representative of the game as we made a lot of mistakes. We had more total offense through the third quarter but we fumbled twice inside the ASU 10-yard line. We also had two interceptions, dropped center snaps, and mishandled pitch outs. There was a 41-yard reception called back by a penalty and another roughing the kicker penalty gave ASU the ball on the SMU 5 which they scored on. It was a poor display, but eventual PAC 10 Champion ASU was too good of a team for us to make that many mistakes. After losing the game our biggest concern was to not let that loss translate into a season deflating loss like the previous year's Arizona debacle.

Our next game September 27 against TCU was moved to the Cotton Bowl in celebration of the Texas Sesquicentennial, our state's 150th birthday. TCU was and is our natural rival. We were similar religiously founded private schools representing our respective ends of the Dallas-Ft. Worth Metroplex: to the west TCU and the east SMU. We were competitive in everything during the seventy-five years since SMU's founding in 1911, but for the last fourteen consecutive years SMU had beaten TCU.

This year we had 431 yards of total offense and won again 31-21 to make it fifteen in a row. Bobby Watters threw for 187 yards and two touchdowns and another rushing while Jeff Atkins ran for 110 yards. Watters was named SWC player of the week for his performance, but it was really our balanced offense that had matured and proven itself.

Our first home game was against a very good Boston College team that would not lose another game after us. We beat them 31-29 in a hard fought game where Watters passed for 180 yards and Atkins continued his rushing success with 129 yards and three touchdowns. Watters and Atkins were on track to be the second tandem to pass for 2000 and rush for 1000 yards in the same season. The first tandem was Chuck Hixson (3,103 yards passing) and Mike Richardson (1,034 yards rushing) in 1968 under Coach Hayden Fry.

We traveled to Baylor as a 3-1 team playing better than most expected. 4-1 Baylor was ranked #13 with only one close loss to a very good USC team. We tried a trick reverse kickoff return that was good for 85 yards and a score in the first fourteen seconds of the game. The last time SMU had scored like that was during our 1982 undefeated season when Bobby Leach took a lateral for a 91 yard winning touchdown against Texas Tech in the final seconds, and Leach became known as the "Miracle Man."

We battled back and forth. Late in the second quarter Watters connected on a series of long passes to set up a touchdown and field goal for a Mustang lead of 24-14 at the half. Baylor battled back in the second half but our defense made key plays and held them off for a final stunning victory 27-21.

Next up was Houston at Texas Stadium. It was a low scoring game that SMU won 10 to 3. The win was good enough to move us up to #18 with a 5-1 record, 4-0 in the conference and tied for first place. It was not supposed to happen, but our team was clicking and we believed we could win the conference.

October 25 we travelled to the University of Texas. Last year we had beaten them at Texas Stadium as badly as they had ever been beaten, 44-14. This year, with a 2-3 record and losses to Stanford, Oklahoma, and Arkansas, Texas was struggling to salvage an imploding season. We were favored, but in Austin hating each other as we did, anything was possible.

The week before the game we began to hear rumors of investigators or something. It was all very hush-hush. The news was unsettling. We didn't know who was involved yet we knew what it could mean. We tried to discount the talk as we looked around the locker room to see if perhaps someone on the team had turned against the rest of us.

Nobody seemed to know anything for sure, but I was told David Stanley was involved. I knew David. He was off the team and nobody knew what he was up to. Whatever it was it wasn't good for SMU. We could hear footsteps again, the footsteps we thought we had left behind.

We put it out of our minds and went down to Austin to play before 65,481 rowdy Texas fans. They held our running game to just forty-eight yards. Meanwhile, Texas put together three scoring drives and had 439 yards of offense to lead 21-0 late in the third quarter. SMU quarterback Bobby Watters ramped up his passing to both Ron Morris and Jeffrey Jacobs and we evened the score at twenty-four with 5:29 to play. On their next drive Texas was forced to punt and we were driving for the win when Watters threw an interception with 2:05 left. That set up the winning Texas field goal with sixteen seconds left in the game for a final score of 27-24.

We had traveled to Austin by bus. That meant a long four hours back. Time enough to think of all the things we could have done differently. A win at Texas would have been important since we had so few things we were playing for. Beating them would have propelled us to our next challenge against #10 Texas A&M and helped us to ignore the rumors that were picking up.

The following week in front of 58,125 standing and screaming fans, Texas A&M beat SMU for their first victory at Texas Stadium. For most of the game it looked like we would beat yet another ranked conference foe. The Aggies trailed SMU four times, twice in the second half. They were down 28-17 in the third quarter but then they rallied in the fourth to take a 32-28 lead. SMU got the ball and drove the field with leaping passes to Ron Morris and option pitches until Morris scored with 7:33 left in the game, 35-32 SMU. With 2:37 in the game A&M had one last chance and scored to take the final lead and the game 39-35. It was a tough loss. The chance of a SWC championship was gone and we could see our season quickly falling apart just like 1985.

The rumors of violations were picking up. On campus it seemed like NCAA investigators were ghosts swirling around, leaving behind whispers of having been there but no real evidence for us to grab on to. Nobody knew anything for sure. We told ourselves that if things were bad our coaches would inform us. Ahead on our schedule were three tough games to close out our season.

The last time we played Notre Dame was in the 1984 Aloha Bowl where SMU won 27-20, but this game would be different. We didn't understand how good Notre Dame was. Yes, they had lost four games but they had only lost by one point each to #2 Michigan and unranked Pittsburgh. Their other two losses were to #2 Alabama and #19 Michigan State. Furthermore, they started 1-4 but had won their last two and regained their footing.

First year head coach Lou Holtz had been a vocal critic of SMU's recruiting practices when he coached at Arkansas from 1977 – 1983. He was unable to beat SMU in his last four attempts and SMU was the primary reason Arkansas couldn't win the SWC outright. As SMU teams beat him, Holtz bitterly complained that the only reason we won was because we cheated. The funny thing about Lou's complaining was that he was responsible for cheating scandals and NCAA probations at four different universities while he was head coach from 1977 – 2004 (University of Arkansas, University of Minnesota, University of Notre Dame and University of South Carolina).

We shouldn't have been listening to the rumors, but we did. We prepared pretty well for Notre Dame but not well enough for the show they were about to put on. Notre Dame's star was a Dallas product out of Woodrow Wilson High School by the name of Tim Brown. This future Heisman Trophy winner seriously considered SMU but chose Notre Dame at the last minute. That decision was costly. Brown had 235 all-purpose yards and two touchdowns against us. We were leading 14-10 early in the second quarter when tailback Jeff Atkins hurt his knee. Notre Dame then caused some fumbles and took advantage of them quickly to make the score 30-14 at the half. In the second half our defense was shaky and the Irish scored thirty-one additional points. The final score was 61-29 Notre Dame. They had 615 yards in total offense and scored more points on us than anybody since Baylor in 1916 (61-0, SMU's second season of football).

Most of us had never experienced anything like this. In four years of high school football I had only lost one close game. At SMU, the worst losses I experienced were the 35-13 end of season loss to eventual national champion Oklahoma in 1985 and the 30-0 loss to #18 ASU in September.

This was something new. Having started the season 5-1 and then lost the last three, we were in real trouble. Sure, two of those were last-second losses but our defense was allowing more and more yards leading up to this 615-yard fiasco. It was both stunning and depressing.

After the Notre Dame whipping we came back to Dallas with our tail between our legs. We were discussing our imploding season when suddenly the conversation changed. Reporters started showing up and asking questions about sanctions and scholarships. We had just lost two tough contests and then gotten blown out by a very good Notre Dame. Things were bad enough. We looked at each other in wonder. Were things about to get worse? No, that was impossible. There was nothing else out there. There couldn't be.

At first there were a few reporters, and then there were a few more. They were elbowing each other, trying to catch the right player to get the right quote. Something was coming. Soon it became obvious. It was a circus, and it was coming to SMU.

Chapter Sixteen:
2011 - Ready to Play

With Scott's help I continued to get stronger, but I wasn't gaining enough weight. He said not to worry and that I was just losing fat and replacing it with muscle. Eventually that would change and the weight gain would come. I had tremendous strength increases the first three months before a series of injuries slowed me down. First was my right hip. It was just bursitis and it went away pretty quickly. Next up was my lower back. We were doing dead lifts and other dangerous lifts and my back painfully tightened. I had muscle spasms that were extremely debilitating. It wouldn't release for months. To work around it, we adjusted our workouts and kept on going. Then my groin went. There wasn't a pop or a sharp pain. It just started hurting. Everyone said it was a sports hernia. So I went back to the Internet. No way was I going to a doctor.

While it didn't say I had cancer, the Internet very clearly said I had a sports hernia...or a groin pull...or a groin strain. With that information in hand I again adjusted my workouts to compensate and tried to push on.

Those back and groin injuries really put me behind schedule. I didn't have enough time as it was, and the leg and back training were critical. The main interruption was to my running and sprint training. I just couldn't do it. I would lay off for a few weeks, then attempt a sprint workout and the pain would come right back. For three solid months I pushed through that pain. Finally it went away. In hindsight, if I had just stopped for six weeks or so it would have healed. But I was too smart for that.

Those injuries caused me to have doubts again. Maybe my buddies who said there was no way I could play again were right. There was a reason why there were no 45-year-olds playing football unless you counted flag football. And quite frankly, my friends who did that got hurt pretty regularly. There are just some things that happen to your body as you age that no amount of training can fix. You can get strong. You can get even stronger than when you were young. But you lose your flexibility. This tightening shows up as pain and injuries to your groin and lower back.

I learned that my back pain was really just my muscles getting stronger and transferring the strain to my tendons. Tendons are more naturally flexible in your youth and then become stiffer as you age. I kept hearing that I needed to stretch and now I know why. I found that as my muscles got stronger they got more painful. Stretching was the only thing that helped.

After about six months of consistent training and stretching, my body released and I had no pain anywhere. I was as ready as I was going to be. With the physical conditioning under control, the next step was re-engaging with SMU athletics.

I knew athletics was no longer what it had been. It was obvious. We had gone from a football factory to a vacant lot to our current position somewhere in between. Recently we were winning again but I didn't think all was well. I wanted a closer look.

Over the years I had maintained great friendships from my SMU days. I started asking around to see who was engaged with athletics. The results were disappointing. Most had moved on. Years of embarrassment and below average football had created tremendous apathy. Sure there were some who were still pissed off at how the program was terminated, but most just didn't care.

Football was always a social thing at SMU. I remember looking up in the stands at the student section where all the guys and girls were mixing and flirting. During a great play or a great game they paid attention, otherwise it was all about socializing. But that didn't bother us, at least they were there. More recently, with the social and the fun parts of our winning football tradition diminished, the desire to go to games and support the team seemed to have vanished. Even though we were playing better and winning again, the support we historically enjoyed did not return to the stands.

Beyond the students and the alumni, I was curious about the athletic support organizations. So I joined the Mustang Club and Lettermen's Association and started going to any and all athletic functions. I discovered something was wrong there too. Most events were lightly attended and without a soul from my generation. At the 2011 Lettermen's BBQ we were to give an Honorary Letter to William Hutchison who was instrumental in keeping football on campus during the troubles. There was a significant number of guys from the pre-Death Penalty years, while there were only a few guys including me, from after. Nobody senior from the Athletic Department or coaching staff was there. The support organizations seemed to be suffering from the same lack of support that our team struggled with.

My wife and I ended up leaving those events early but I made a commitment to continue to be more involved, and to try to get my generation more active regardless if they let me play.

I was starting to understand how much destruction the school had absorbed. And it wasn't just the team. The penalty had touched everything and its effects were still lingering. It wasn't fair. My mind wandered. How was SMU going to break loose from this long-standing curse?

Scott continued to push me and I pushed myself harder. Suddenly I looked up and it was almost August. SMU's practices were starting soon and my injuries had just barely healed. I achieved almost all of my goals and could bench press 225 pounds twenty-seven times. I was able to leg press sets of 900 pounds. I weighed 272 pounds and my body fat was down to 16%. Now for the big test. Speed. I had to run a 4.8 second 40-yard dash.

I went out to the practice field with Scott. After warming up and stretching, I felt good. Scott signaled "Go" and I ran. This was it. All of the injuries and all of the training, came down to a handful of seconds. As I crossed the line I wondered what it was. Scott looked down and appeared to be frowning. I walked over and he showed me...4.76 seconds. I did it. All of the hard work paid off. I had reached the standards for college defensive ends that received invitations to compete in the NFL Combine.

I lost twenty to thirty pounds of fat and replaced it with thirty to forty pounds of muscle in eight months and I regained my speed. I was in as good or better physical shape as when I was twenty-one. Scott's core workouts and modern training gave me the foundation I hadn't had in college. I was ready to try out for the SMU football team. The question was, would they let me?

Chapter Seventeen:
1986 - The WFAA Show

Wednesday November 12, 1986 four days after the Notre Dame loss, WFAA was going to air a story about SMU football. Rumors had been swirling around the locker room for weeks. Those rumors intensified to the point where it was affecting our play. Before the rumors began we were 5-1, tied for first in the SWC, and ranked #18. After the rumors started we lost three straight and were obviously unranked. There were two games left, and we could still salvage a winning and honorable season if we could get our heads back on.

We knew there had been an interview with Coach Collins on campus alleging more violations. We didn't know how well SMU had handled it or specific details. WFAA was running promotions about their big story, so we had a pretty good idea they thought it was important. The media circus was beginning to set up, they were preparing and knew we were about to take a hit.

I sat in front of my TV and tuned in to Channel 8. It was investigative reporter John Sparks' story and he had done all the work, but Dale Hansen, WFAA's Sports Director, took control of it. Sparks was a UT graduate and football booster. Obviously that would look bad. Hansen was the perfect addition to the story. He graduated high school in 1968 with the

Vietnam War raging. He enlisted in the Navy and got his high school girlfriend pregnant. After the Navy he drifted from one job to the next, first in sales for a finance company and then as a bill collector for a hospital. Eventually he enrolled in a vocational school for broadcasting and started his sports casting career. He was from the mid-west and had no college affiliation. With Hansen in the lead, it would be more difficult to allege that the UT-run WFAA was out to get an SMU that kept out-recruiting and beating Texas on the football field.

Hansen opened with a brief history of the SMU football program and its current probation. Then he started in with a story about former SMU linebacker David Stanley. Stanley said that an SMU booster paid him $25,000 to attend SMU in 1983 and that he received $400 and his mother an additional $350 per month for living expenses while he was enrolled through December 1985. The accusations sounded bad.

Dale Hansen continued with the story setup. On October 27 Hansen and Sparks taped an interview with SMU Head Coach Bobby Collins, Athletic Director Bob Hitch, and Associate Athletic Director Henry Lee Parker. The three were told of Stanley's accusations and asked for their responses. They had no response other than an awkward, embarrassing silence. Then Hansen produced an official SMU envelope addressed to Stanley's mother and said it contained money from Parker. He pointed out the initials 'H.L.P." printed in the return address and asked if they were his initials. Parker initially said "Yes," but then backtracked saying "No, he didn't write that way."

Too late in the interview, Bob Hitch tried to turn it around and argue that it was disappointing to him that the newsmen would take the word of a dropout and drug addict over the three administrators. It was a nightmare. SMU not only looked bad, we looked guilty.

Administrators had promised the SMU community that all of our previous problems were the fault of boosters. Now it was exposed that they knowingly lied. There was no denying it. Everyone could see the guilt and the lies with their very own eyes. The imagery of that interview shattered what was left of SMU community support.

Reporters descended; they were suffocating. This was no mud show, this was the big one and every reporter wanted his scoop. Two days later, the Dallas Morning News ran a story about our starting tight end Albert Reese that alleged he was living rent-free in a Dallas apartment. The apartment was supposedly being provided by an SMU booster. He later showed his lease but it didn't matter. The reporters were loosed and giving chase.

Chapter Eighteen:
1986 - End of Season

In the midst of the expanding scandal, we caught a break. Three days after the WFAA show, we had an away game against Texas Tech. Traveling to Lubbock allowed us an escape for just a little while. We practiced hard and tried to forget all the potential problems that laid ahead. Texas Tech was 6-3 and had won four in a row. They were playing for a bid in the Independence Bowl and were motivated to win. We were 5-4, in a slump, and had just taken what most thought was a knock-out punch.

The game wouldn't appear on TV, few fans would travel or support us, and there was no chance to win a trophy. Everyone was convinced we were corrupt and we were facing the termination of our entire team. The 1986 season had always been about pride, but now we would find out if we were quitters.

Jones Stadium in Lubbock was hostile and loud. Our starting running back Jeff Atkins traveled with the team but was hurt and couldn't play. Our starting tight end Albert Reese was ordered to sit out due to the free rent allegations. Through all the adversity of the previous weeks and through what was to come, we knew this was a test. It was a test of our character and our ability to overcome the smothering anger and the chaos.

The game was a defensive struggle. Our defense, which played so poorly the previous few weeks showed up. We caused seven fumbles and recovered five of them. Our offense moved the ball well enough and was able to control the clock. We scored a touchdown on a 47-yard pass to Ron Morris and kicker Brandee Brownlee hit two field goals out of four attempts for a 13-0 lead in the fourth quarter. Tech scored a touchdown and then converted on a fake punt to the SMU 31 with seven minutes left. On the next pass play, we knocked the ball loose and recovered. From there, we moved the ball well enough to eat up the remaining seven minutes of the game and barely won 13-7.

It was an unimpressive win in yardage gained or points scored, but our defense had won the game for us and in doing so, showed their ability to overcome the previous few let-downs. Head Coach Bobby Collins was given the game ball and carried to midfield as if we had just won the Cotton Bowl. That was obviously not the case, but at 6-4 we had secured a winning season, we had proven we were still a team, and we had shown that we "weren't dead yet."

Once we arrived back in Dallas, any emotional high we had came crashing down. The scandal had gone national. We were off balance as the reporters kept digging and harassing us. The whole thing was coming apart and we had one more game against #9 Arkansas in Texas Stadium.

Practices from that week remain a blur. I'm sure we did practice. I'm sure we watched film and prepared. I just don't remember it. I do remember that the drumbeat contin-ued to get louder, and rumors of a guaranteed imposition of the Death Penalty were rapidly taking over our conversations.

My teammates and I had questions. What happened to a player when the penalty was imposed? How many years of eligibility did each of us have and how would that be affected? What would happen to the coaches?

I'm sure at some point we were concerned about playing a very good Arkansas team but as I mentioned, I don't remember any of it.

Meanwhile, the hits just kept on coming.

On Wednesday November 19, three days before our game, two hundred SMU professors submitted a petition calling for the end of "quasi-professional athletics." They wanted a ban on athletic scholarships.

On Friday November 21, the day before our game, SMU President L. Donald Shields resigned. He cited stress and deteriorating health exacerbated by his preexisting diabetes.

On Saturday November 22, we played our last game as Mustangs. On some subconscious level we all knew it. I remember thinking there would be some last minute exemption or a lack of evidence and it would all just magically disappear. I had turned twenty-one the week before and I remember having such childish thoughts as I looked through the hole in the roof of Texas Stadium. But that's all they were, childish thoughts.

There would be no savior and no heavenly ending. Arkansas was a very good team but had never beaten SMU at Texas Stadium. They had two losses in conference and still had a chance at the Cotton Bowl if Texas A&M would stumble against Texas five days later. Arkansas needed to beat us to even have a prayer. We knew they would have no sympathy for what we were going through.

Under the glare of the media, having lost the support of the SMU community and watching the NCAA circle ever closer, we knew we were done. The coaches spoke of our season in the past tense. They prepared us for the game by talking about the significance of the moment and how we as a team held together.

We ran onto the field and tried. But we were off just a step and nothing seemed to work. Arkansas didn't waver. They came out, they made their plays, and then they administered the coup de grace to put us out of our misery. The final score was 41-0 (our worst loss in twenty-two years against a conference foe and our first shutout in Texas Stadium).

Following the Arkansas loss, we had our regular Monday postseason team meeting November 24. Coach Collins was there of course. It was different in that AD Bob Hitch was there but we covered the normal things a coach tells his players after a season's end. We did some things well. We did some things poorly. We played as a team and showed heart to play through all the drama. We needed to study hard and get good grades. He did not discuss the future of our team or either his or Hitch's future with the team. They didn't discuss the pending investigation. They just told us they would keep us apprised of what happened.

Coach Collins was a reserved man and hard to know. He expected his position coaches to manage us players, and then he managed them. His pregame speeches were always the same as he talked about us "doing our jobs" and "taking care of business out there." We never doubted he cared about us as more than just players and he never said negative things about any of us despite the pressure to do so. He quietly took the criticism and encouraged us to be better.

It had been the longest season with the most distractions and less to play for than any team in college football history. And yet we finished 6-5. Our schedule featured six teams that went to bowl games, not to mention the always tough Notre Dame. We played with only seventy-one scholarship players (twenty-four fewer than all of our opponents) and posted our seventh consecutive winning season as Mustangs. It could have been much worse.

Even though we could see what was coming, we never gave up until the Arkansas game. Quarterback Bobby Watters threw for 2,041 yards and became the third SMU quarterback to throw more than 2,000 yards in a season. Because of injuries towards the end of the season, Jeff Atkins didn't reach 1,000 yards rushing but he ran for 3,260 yards and moved to ninth in career rushing at SMU. And receiver Ron Morris caught a season high 757 yards with six touchdowns to become fourth on the SMU all-time receiving list.

For the class of 1983 it really was over. That class came to SMU as the sixth best recruiting class in the country. They came in as the younger players that were going to continue the Mustang dynasty and win multiple Southwest Conference and even national championships. It didn't happen. For a senior class that had so much potential, the last game of the season and their careers was supposed to be a special memory. It was not supposed to be a shutout at home. Those guys were champions and I had looked up to them. It had been a long and difficult road, but now they could at last crack a bit of a smile. They weren't happy it was over; they were relieved.

Eleven days later on Friday December 5, SMU allowed Coach Bobby Collins and Athletic Director Bob Hitch to resign. All nine members of Coach Collin's staff were informed that their contracts would not be renewed in June and six had already left and found new coaching jobs. That didn't control the madness; it only led to more confusion.

For us younger players, it wasn't over. The next chapter was about to begin and it would not be like the last one. This time we would have no coaches, no athletic director, no president, and no board of governors or leaders to help smooth the way. We were on our own, drifting, expecting the final NCAA hammer to fall. Our date with the NCAA loomed, we just had to wait for it.

Chapter Nineteen:
2011 - Obstacles

At forty-five years old, I felt like a football player. My body had regained the quickness and the strength I had in my youth. I thought it was at least physically possible to play again.

After the initial meeting with my friend Mike Shore in February and his positive feedback from SMU AD Steve Orsini, I was optimistic. Then it occurred to me that perhaps I needed to make sure I still had those two years of eligibility. I had previously joked about it, but truthfully I had never re-searched it.

In March, I called the NCAA and spoke to a nice lady in their compliance department. I explained who I was and what I wanted. She paused for a moment, collected her thoughts then said I didn't have any eligibility due to the "five year rule."

My heart stopped for a moment.

She said that once I started playing football in 1984, my five-year time limit started and therefore my eligibility expired in 1989. I mentioned the Death Penalty and how the NCAA ended my career for me. She told me that was not a legitimate excuse.

Wow…so that was it. My quest was over before it really began. The dream just vanished.

She did tell me that the NCAA bylaws were online and that I could look them up myself. After bumming around a bit, I took her up on her suggestion and decided to read about this five-year rule. After all, I had told enough people about my quest that I needed to be sure.

She was correct. I read it in black and white. She didn't get into the details though and she didn't tell me about the section that referenced exceptions. In that section, there were many exceptions that allowed a player more time. The main component of these exceptions was the concept of "control." If something happened to disrupt an athlete's five-year clock that was "out of his control" he could get an exception. The examples they used were pregnancy, military draft, financial and health issues, along with something titled "special circumstances."

Well hell! If the Death Penalty imposed on me by these very same NCAA folks was not the poster child definition of a "special circumstance out of my control" I didn't know what was. I called her back and said I understood their position, but I disagreed and I wanted a case number for further action.

I got one and continued forward. I soon found out that I was not alone. The NCAA has a standing committee that hears hundreds of cases a year for athletic eligibility re-instatement. The head of that committee is Jennifer Henderson. I contacted her about my case explaining everything. I politely told her that I believed my loss of eligibility was clearly "out of my control." I wanted a hearing and a vote of her committee on the issue. Now we would see the wheels of justice turn. After all, the NCAA was there for the student-athlete, it said so right on their website.

She considered my comments and then she told me that my eligibility expired due to the five-year rule. I held my tongue because I had already been down that track. Then she tossed me a new hurdle. She said that since the NCAA allowed us players to transfer to another school after the penalty, my decision to stay at SMU and graduate constituted my control of the situation. I listened, considered her comments, then told her I still disagreed and wanted a vote of her committee. She said "No" and this is where things got interesting.

The NCAA sells itself as an athletic body that supports academics. In 1987, I chose to stay at SMU and graduate as opposed to transferring away to play football and jeopardizing my education.

From the NCAA's own website, it states:

"THE NCAA's CORE PURPOSE IS TO govern competition in a fair, safe, equitable and sportsmanlike manner, and to integrate intercollegiate athletics into higher education so that the educational experience of the student-athlete is paramount."

Hmmmmm. *The educational experience of the student-athlete is paramount.* I sacrificed my athletic eligibility in 1987 to stay at SMU and pursued my degree. I think that counted as treating my educational experience as paramount. And yet I was being penalized for this decision. I wanted an NCAA vote to tell me whether or not I should have risked my education and left SMU to play football somewhere else. Surely the NCAA would not say that I should have transferred simply to play football. Surely that's not what they believed.

If I forced a vote and they voted against reinstating my eligibility, they would be telling me that I made the wrong decision in 1987; that I should have transferred to play football and that athletics, not academics was actually paramount. This would leave their imposed penalty on me but would corrupt their own Core Purpose. The NCAA would then have to change their purpose to read something like "...so that the educational experience of the student-athlete is *almost as important as athletics.*"

100

On the other hand if they voted to reinstate my eligibility and allowed me to play, they would be telling me that I made the right decision in 1987 to pursue academics because academics was paramount and would be consistent with their Core Purpose.

In either case I was fascinated by the prospect that it was *they* and not *I* who was in control. I had no role in the infractions. They imposed the penalty ending football on SMU and me, and now they were saying I was in control. The only control I had was in choosing what to lose: academics or athletics. They made me a loser either way.

All I wanted was clarity on this issue and a vote from the committee seemed a good way to get it. When I pushed Ms. Henderson again, she then deferred to the fact that I had no standing to ask for a vote.

No standing? How could they penalize me and then tell me that I had no rights? This seemed patently unfair and even illegal.

Then I was informed that the NCAA was a private organization made up of member institutions like SMU and not subject to due process. As such, only member institutions had standing and the ability to ask for a vote. Basically to the NCAA I didn't exist and I don't exist. That was why they always won in court when an individual student-athlete challenged them. Over and over courts deferred to the NCAA itself as the best interpreter of its own bylaws. They seemed subject to federal oversight only on issues of discrimination like age, gender, and race.

Ms. Henderson obviously knew I had no ability to pursue them so she directed me back to a member organization. She said that my relationship was with SMU and not the NCAA. I needed to take it up with them if I wanted to pursue my eligibility.

That was a tough one. I had no issue with SMU. When the Death Penalty was imposed, SMU could have cut my scholarship and left me to the fates. Instead they continued to honor my scholarship and I was able to earn two degrees from them. SMU didn't harm me. If anything, the school helped and protected me. I was not going to sue them so I could get a vote with the NCAA. I thanked Ms. Henderson and hung up.

I thought about all this. My only recourse was to persuade SMU to file a request with the NCAA on my behalf. I checked on how that worked. The procedure involved the SMU Compliance Department filling out a *Waiver for Student Athlete Re-instatement* and submitting it to the NCAA. Apparently it was quite detailed. I discovered that each one filled out by a compliance officer represented hundreds of man-hours to prepare. The compliance office did not fill out those forms unprompted; they didn't have that kind of time. It had to be for someone important. I kept digging.

I found out the head coach of a sport directed the compliance office to file the request. The compliance office checked the NCAA bylaws for applicable rules and possible exceptions, prepared the waiver, and got the signature of a head coach, athletic director, or school president for submission. Once submitted, the NCAA committee acted fairly quickly, as they only had thirty days to reject the waiver or it was accepted by default.

I called the SMU Compliance office identified myself and told them what I wanted to do. They called the NCAA for clarification, probably talked to the same person I did, and then read to me chapter and verse what the NCAA officer had read to me before. That didn't help. I already knew what the bylaws said. I was pursuing an exception. By definition an exception had to go to the committee for a vote. My circumstance wasn't in the book and I couldn't find any reference to Death Penalty exceptions in their bylaws. They were going to have to make a determination: was the Death Penalty an "in control" or "out of control" event for a student-athlete like me?

I could tell the hundreds of man hours to complete the form would be a real impediment and thought if I could make it easy for the compliance department, perhaps they would give it the old college try. What I needed was a lawyer to help put the waiver together. Not just any lawyer, but a litigator. Someone who went to trial and argued, convinced others of his arguments, and won.

Many of my best friends were lawyers and one in particular was among the best litigators in Dallas. He was a partner and head of the Dallas litigation department at one of the biggest firms in Texas, Vinson & Elkins. He did not go to SMU and had no bias in the case. He would tell me if I was wasting my time and if it was worth the effort. John Wander was the guy I needed to see.

John was a huge sports fan and he quickly agreed to look into my case. Together we went over the NCAA Manual. After listening to me and reviewing the bylaws, he agreed that my argument had merits and was worth pursuing. He was too expensive for me to pay his hourly rate and he told me that his time was too valuable to waste if the case was a loser. But he was interested and agreed to devote some man-hours on research to complete the waiver for me anyway. I hoped this would sway the SMU compliance office when I showed them it was a no-lose proposition for them. I would do the research and fill out the waiver. All they had to do was send it up.

There was one other piece of the puzzle. I needed the head coach to sign the request and offer me a roster spot. Technically, an athletic director or school president could sign it. But in practical terms only a head coach could offer a spot on his team. Simply put, it was no coach no waiver, and no waiver no vote.

It was early April; I called SMU's on-campus recruiting coach, Steve Stigall. His voice greeting said that due to NCAA rules he couldn't call back anybody that was a recruit or who might be calling on behalf of a recruit. They were in the blackout period where coaches were held to very stringent rules about talking to potential recruits. This was a new wrinkle. What was I?

Well, I was an SMU alumnus which meant it was okay to talk to me, but I was also attempting to regain my eligibility and could therefore be considered a recruit. If I was a recruit he couldn't talk to me. I left a message but he didn't call me back. I tried him a few more times and finally caught him a week or two later. We had a nice conversation during which he admitted that he had never heard of a situation like mine and had no idea if I was a recruit or not. He offered to get clarification from the compliance department and call me back.

When he called, he said compliance told him that they had talked to the NCAA and that I didn't have eligibility. He said the five-year rule applied to me and my eligibility was up in 1989. I already knew that. That was the fourth time I had been read a page out of the NCAA Manual. I explained that there were exceptions and I was trying to access the exception process. He suggested I talk to Coach Randy Ross who was the Director of Football Operations. Coach Ross was a good old boy. He had been coaching a long time and had been with SMU since 2006. Before that he was with Alabama for seventeen years.

I talked to Coach Ross. He was great, he was personable, he was supportive of former SMU athletes, but he had no idea what to do with me. When we met at his office we discussed what I was trying to do and it was obvious he didn't believe I could do it. I told him I just wanted support to get the waiver filed and thus a vote with the NCAA. If I got my eligibility restored I offered to "try out" for the team. If they thought I could do it, I was prepared to pay my own tuition and walk-on to the team. I would cost them nothing. If they felt I couldn't physically handle playing, we would shake hands and call it a day. All I wanted was that NCAA vote. He agreed to check further.

In the meantime, I figured I needed Head Coach June Jones to know that I was serious. My name and strange quest had been brought up in SMU meetings but he didn't know anything about me or why I was trying to play again. I'm sure he thought I was crazy just like everyone else, but he was supposed to be an innovative and quirky coach. I wanted to see how innovative he was.

My best friend from our SMU playing days was David Richards. David played in the NFL for a dozen years or so and actually played for Coach Jones with the Atlanta Falcons. He and I had maintained our friendship personally and professionally over the years so it was an easy call to ask David to contact Coach Jones on my behalf. Not only did David play in the NFL under Coach Jones, but since Jones moved to Dallas and began coaching at SMU they had re-established their relationship. When I called David he laughed and told me I was crazy. I expected that. But he said he loved me and would support me even though it was nuts and I would get hurt.

My wife had gotten to him too.

I then asked him the same thing I had asked Scott, my trainer. If he had no injuries and felt he could do it, wouldn't he go back for one more season? David was a competitive athlete through and through. He said he would give anything to be pain-free and play just one more game. He called Jones on my behalf.

When David called me back a week or so later after talking with Coach Jones he said he told him all about me, that I was a dear friend of SMU, and that he should meet me. He said Jones agreed. But the clock was against me now. The coaches were deep into their work preparing for the upcoming season. They didn't have much time for a wild card like me. I tried but couldn't set a meeting with Coach Jones. His assistant told me to be patient. First he was in California for a week to look at recruits, then he was in Tahiti for his foundation and football camps. And then he was on vacation in Hawaii before his coaching duties began again.

While I waited for Jones to come back in town and meet with me, I continued to talk with Coach Ross who informed me Jones knew all about me but had not decided what he was going to do. He felt it was a compliance issue mainly and that I should go back to them.

My main argument continued to bore into the five-year rule and the issue of control. I felt that the NCAA needed to make a ruling specific to the Death Penalty and in fact all penalties levied by the NCAA that affected innocent student-athletes.

Over and over I read the NCAA bylaws. I kept thinking I would read some new sentence or rule that I missed. I kept thinking there was some exception that applied to me. The rules kept coming back the same. The NCAA attorneys had written and re-written the rule book numerous times to manage every possible contingency. They didn't want any surprises and made sure there weren't any. But then I saw it; a sub-heading to the five-year rule that I read numerous times and yet missed its significance. There *was* an exception that applied specifically to my situation. I hurriedly picked up the phone to see what my lawyer thought.

Chapter Twenty:
Coach Jones' Answer

Wander listened carefully as I outlined the new exception. He asked a few questions and pondered it all.

The particular rule stated that if a student-athlete had eligibility (which I did through 1989 under the five-year rule), and his last season had not crossed the halfway mark, he or she was entitled to a standalone sixth year of eligibility. The special exceptions that applied were: injuries, financial hardship, or the member institution dropping the sport. I had read about medical and personal hardships giving an athlete a "sixth" year but I never heard of the exception due to a school dropping a sport.

I thought I was due a general exception to the five-year rule, but I liked this even better. I was entitled to a sixth year regardless of my five-year eligibility clock. I was entitled to a sixth year regardless of their ruling on "control." I was entitled to a sixth year because SMU dropped football while I still had eligibility.

The NCAA's Death Penalty was only for one year, 1987. It was SMU that terminated the season for 1988 because of the harsh restrictions imposed on us. SMU cancelled the program long before the halfway mark of my last season. In fact, they cancelled it the year before it began.

This NCAA exception was not written in anticipation of my situation, but who cared? They imposed the penalty on me, they caused SMU to drop the program affecting me, and they wrote the rules allowing me back in. It fit and I wanted it.

After the meeting with John I was encouraged. We wrote up my new argument and cited the specific bylaws and exceptions that applied. We were no longer asking for an interpretation, we were arguing facts. I presented the new argument to the Director of the SMU Compliance Department. I heard back from his boss. She indicated that while she appreciated the research, without Coach Jones' direct support for me on his team the SMU Compliance Department would do nothing.

Actually, that was great news. I was now done with the compliance department. The decision on submitting a waiver to the NCAA would all come down to the head coach and what he wanted to do. I had the last remaining hurdle staring me in the face and it was Coach June Jones.

Coach Jones was a very hard man to catch. As the days ticked by, I continued working out. I felt great but knew I was running out of time. I was deep into the summer months now. Jones knew about my quest, he knew how to contact me if he was interested and he hadn't. I started to get a bad feeling. The answer to whether or not Coach Jones wanted me on his team was clear. The answer was "No."

But I did what I had done for eight months and kept at it. Making the team was about more than playing college football again and getting in shape at age forty-five. It was about telling my daughter that I had done nothing wrong when I played in the 1980's. It was about healing a still open wound from an unfairly imposed penalty. It was bigger than me.

On the other hand, I knew it had always been a long shot. Coach Jones indicated a concern for my health. His coaches mentioned the fact that I hadn't played competitively for twenty-five years. The 2011 team was filled with seniors that had played for him for three years. This season was supposed to be a signature season for the post-Death Penalty Mustangs. Into all this, a forty-five-year-old player from the old days would be a distraction. Did they really want to bring up all those old memories just as SMU was poised to break free? Probably not, but everything I ever read about Coach Jones told me he was just creative enough to consider it. He took risks. He believed in second chances, and I was a second chance. I kept pushing.

On August 1, I got the final answer. It was Coach Ross. Practices were starting the following week. My pulse quickened. "Yes?" Coach Jones was in town and it was time to finish this. Coach Ross had some news for me. "Yes?" He told me that he had been specifically tasked with informing me that Coach Jones was *not* going to support my waiver. My stomach churned and my shoulders slumped. We talked for half an hour but he kept repeating that he was only authorized to tell me that Jones wouldn't support my waiver.

I still wanted my face-to-face with Jones; I wanted him to say "No" to me directly. He had never met with me and I was an unknown quantity to him. He didn't know my motivations. He didn't know if I was hostile to SMU from what had happened back in the 80's. I understood all that. But I questioned whether he understood why my generation was gone and that I might have...ahhh...what was the use? Nobody really cared then or now about what happened to us, and I moved to accept that it was over.

I arranged a time to meet with Coach Jones anyway. It was what I would call a walk and talk. He carved out a bit of time and I got to say a few things. The purpose of the meeting for me was to look him in the eye and let him know I could have done it. His answer was still "No." I tried to stay professional and cordial, though I was disappointed. I decided not to pressure him for *the* reason he said no. There were a lot of reasons and one specifically didn't matter. It was his team, his decision, and I respected that. I thanked him for his consideration and told him that I understood his decision. I told him I had been serious about playing and worked hard at it. We shook hands and I said I would see him around. And that was that.

As I walked back to my car, a lot of thoughts tumbled through my mind. I really did understand his position. Quite frankly, if I were the coach I would have probably said no too. The Death Penalty was a nasty subject and it was risky to bring it up. It was probably best to get rid of anything from that time. That was me. I had just been gotten rid of.

My friends were not so understanding. Over the last few months, they had seen my determination and gotten excited for me. They encouraged me to continue the quest. Any college could file the waiver to restore my eligibility. They suggested I try to play for TCU or Baylor. Maybe I could trek up to Denton and North Texas University. Surely some coach would give me the chance. I considered all those options. My vanity smiled. It was tempting and it did seem a waste not to try. But I didn't want to just play football again. I wanted to play for SMU again. The idea of wearing TCU purple and playing against SMU was a bridge too far. I wouldn't risk getting hurt, paying thousands of dollars in unnecessary tuition, or compromising my SMU relationships just to have my "senior" year of football. I needed more. I felt it was SMU or nothing.

So that was it. Eight months of working out and research and interaction with the NCAA and SMU coaches and compliance officers, and it was over. I failed. I took a few weeks off from working out to consider what I had gone through. True, I was disappointed but the disappointment hit me in dribs and drabs and not all at once. As I kept confronting obstacles, suddenly a path forward would appear. The whole process had been a rollercoaster.

When I reviewed the pros and cons, I found that I only had a couple of cons. The biggest of course was that I failed.

110

The pros were overwhelming. I got in great shape. Yes, I was now too big to be a forty-five year-old former athlete but I could change my workouts and get back down to a muscular 245 pounds. I was eating better and drinking less. My wife was fully supportive and encouraging of my new physicality. We joked about how bad I looked before my training regimen.

In hindsight it wasn't so funny. I was on track for an early death. Looking around at my peer group we all needed to be cutting back on the alcohol and controlling our weight. I didn't see it before but alcohol begins to kill you in your forties to the point that in your fifties, you're a goner.

I made new friends. My trainer Scott has become a great friend. I met dozens of new friends from the gym and these friends have led to more business and social opportunities. Existing friends noticed my workouts and a number of them have started to get back in shape too.

I also got more involved and invested in SMU. While I had great friends from my days at SMU, for the most part they were friends that had nothing to do with athletics. I had had no involvement with the institution itself, and now for the first time, I was a member of the Lettermen's Association. I started going to their events and meeting their members.

I finally bought that SMU flag and put it up on my house. If I was going to commit to SMU, I had to have a flag no matter how they played.

I bought a sports package to receive SMU away games on TV and started watching the team play. I had been married thirteen years and never watched an SMU game. My wife wondered who I was.

The more I did, the more I wanted to do. I started to realize that I missed not supporting my school. I missed not having a team to root for.

Through this experience I learned that I still cared deeply about SMU and my time there. I found pride in my time playing football despite what happened to our team. I talked to former teammates and learned that they too felt disconnected from SMU because of the penalty and its aftermath. I found that even though Coach Jones wouldn't support the re-instatement of my eligibility with the NCAA, I wasn't done with SMU. I was becoming more interested in engaging after twenty-five years of avoidance.

So, there I was. I was involved and I was officially an SMU Mustang again. At social events I engaged in college football talk. I talked about other teams and I talked about SMU. When people brought up the Death Penalty, I answered their questions directly rather than avoiding them like the past. "Yeah, we cheated," "No, I didn't," and "Yes, all the good teams were doing it."

Now that I was engaging in college sports conversations, I was getting sucked into all kinds of arguments about what constituted cheating, why the SWC had broken up, and why players weren't allowed to get paid. On and on it went.

I continued to have nagging questions about my experiences that I couldn't answer. Questions like: What was the NCAA and how did they get so much power over the schools and players? Why did SMU participate in this system? How were cheating teams like Texas avoiding what SMU couldn't? I wanted to know everything about college football and how it evolved to where it is today. I wanted to know how the NCAA was able to penalize me in 1987, tell me I didn't exist to them, and that I had no rights then or now.

Since Coach Jones turned me down, I had some unexpected free time. So I decided to research college football, where the NCAA came from, and how they got the power to prevent me from playing again. Then, I decided I wanted to know exactly what had happened to me and my team in 1987. I thought maybe I could come up with answers that would satisfy all my new questions. In doing so, I thought I could better answer Amanda's big one, did I do anything wrong?

Chapter Twenty-One:
Birth of College Football and NCAA

It was 1827. The rules were simple and few. At universities and colleges out east, a mob of men formed on a field one afternoon and launched into each other. Violence and injuries were common. A player wasn't down simply because he was on the ground. He could crawl with the ball while opposing players kicked and punched at him savagely until he cried "down." It was brutal yet people paid to watch this. Sure it was fun, unless you were the guy getting kicked on the ground.

These early games were nothing more than large mobs trying to move the ball to the goal area. The players were supposedly students at the colleges and universities, yet no one checked any ID's. From the start, amateurism in college football was preached more than it was practiced. With few referees and fewer rules, cheating was rampant. Phantom "students" played for different teams as needed. But they didn't play for free. They had to be paid to take this kind of punishment.

Soon, slush funds were set up to pay their "students" and the game grew. It remained violent by design; with more violence, came more fans and more money. With more money, came more cheating to get better players. Underlying all this was the mayhem the game produced. Harvard started a tradition of "Bloody Monday" where the freshmen played the sophomores. At these games blood was definitely spilled. In fact, the violence was so bad that by 1861, both Harvard and Yale banned all forms of football. But the game just wouldn't die.

In 1873, Columbia, Rutgers, Princeton and Yale met in New York City to establish the first set of intercollegiate football rules. Walter Camp, a first-rate player for Yale, suggested changes to the game such as reducing the players on each side from fifteen to eleven which opened up the game and emphasized speed over strength. He also suggested creating a line of scrimmage, adding the snap of the ball from the center to the quarterback, and adopting the forward pass. It took several years for these changes to be implemented, but they revolutionized the game. Colleges and universities began picking up the sport in large numbers.

The games were not officially part of the colleges. They were club sports made up of "students" from their respective schools. It grew fast and spread beyond the east coast schools that invented the game so that by 1895, the Big Ten Conference was created in the Midwestern states.

In 1892, the concept of scholarships was born at the University of Chicago. The University actually called them *student service payments* and paid good money to get players. It wasn't long before they created a football powerhouse and athletic department that brought large sums of money into the university's bank account. The winning and the money caught the attention of other universities who soon emulated Chicago.

Certain formations like the flying wedge caused a large number of offensive players to crash into large numbers of defensive players. In one game in 1894, the Hampden Park Blood Bath caused at least four crippling injuries. In other games, players were actually dying. In 1905, nineteen college players nationwide died. In addition to those deaths, forty-six high school students died that year as a result of football injuries. President Roosevelt threatened to shut the game down if drastic changes weren't made. The universities wrung their hands and wondered what they could do.

The lack of reform in football programs was due to the fact that the faculty and administrators were not really in charge. Students managed the clubs, hired the coaches, and organized the contests. And who guided them? At many schools it was not members of the faculty, who were either disinterested or openly hostile. It was not the administrators, who could do little to oversee student clubs that were financially independent. It was largely the alumni that stepped into this role, donating their time, experience, and money. Some had been athletes during their own college days and wanted to help out the latest generation; others were attracted by a chance to be part of the excitement. Since colleges lacked meaningful control of these clubs at their own institutions, school presidents thought one way to regain some influence was for them to form an association to oversee intercollegiate athletics.

What they needed was an organization to make sure the rules were being followed and injuries were reduced. They needed something to stop the deaths. With President Roosevelt's push, sixty-two colleges and universities created the Intercollegiate Athletic Association of the United States in 1905. Its initial mission was "to protect young people from the dangerous and exploitative athletics practices of the time." This organization did not touch or have anything to do with money or scholarships awarded to athletes so long as the players were students. The organization was more concerned with exerting control over competition and championship games and tournaments. After all, that was what the President wanted: to stop the injuries and death, not the game itself.

It was a weak organization without any real power or independent source of funds. They largely issued appeals to amateurism that were ignored. In 1910, the IAAUS changed its name to the National Collegiate Athletic Association or NCAA. For the next forty years, the NCAA existed mainly as a forum for sharing resumes and gossiping about college athletics. The NCAA's bylaws structured sports but provided no enforcement. They espoused amateurism yet did nothing more than talk of it. In fact, membership in the NCAA did not even require the following of its bylaws.

After going to the effort to create an organization to deal with one problem (violence in football), the members immediately began to focus on other issues of mutual concern such as amateurism. Interestingly, the rules on amateurism were not concerned with colleges profiting from athletics. They were only concerned with preventing students from doing so. In 1922, the members unanimously adopted a *Ten Point Code of Eligibility* which forbade any payments to students for their participation in sports, including athletic scholarships.

In 1929, the Carnegie Foundation issued a report "American College Athletics" which concluded that the recruitment of football players had reached a state of "nationwide commerce." The report documented widespread subsidies to athletes and improper recruiting. Out of 112 universities they examined, payments to athletes occurred at 81, and at 61 of those, multiple groups (administration, alumni, and athletic association) were involved. Clearly, the majority of colleges were not following NCAA guidelines. Schools had open payrolls, no-show jobs, and slush funds. They made no apologies for funding their teams and the teams themselves made no attempt to hide the payrolls. In fact, in 1939 freshman players at the University of Pittsburgh went on strike because they were getting paid less than the upperclassmen were.

To bring payments to players out in the open, in 1935 the Southeastern Conference became the first to offer athletic scholarships. To compete with the SEC soon other conferences offered athletic scholarships too. Conferences made these decisions and had more influence than the toothless NCAA. The NCAA tried to avoid the impression it had lost control of college sports so they grudgingly allowed athletic scholarships but only under institutional control and oversight.

In 1948 the NCAA again attempted to prohibit all concealed and indirect benefits for college athletes. In essence, they wanted to shine a light on the hidden payments and end them. Further, they wanted all monies going to players to now be awarded as scholarships and based solely on financial need. It was called the "Sanity Code" and had the penalty of expulsion from the NCAA if violated. Schools rebelled at penalizing each other. Everyone knew players had to be paid or they wouldn't play. That was a basic concept with any business and certainly collegiate football was huge business. The Sanity Code was repealed a few years later after everyone ignored it.

The debate within the NCAA on athletic scholarships continued until 1953 when the association approved them across the board. For many, this crucial move marked the shift from amateurism to professionalism. The Ivy League, founders of college sports, refused to give athletic scholarships calling it "pay for play" and began to deemphasize their sports programs.

Most of the conferences had already been offering athletic scholarships, so the NCAA just codified what was already their policy. The Big Ten Conference refused until 1961, when they finally gave in to competitive pressures and began granting athletic scholarships too.

No longer could the older and richer programs expect the best players to enroll in their schools based solely on tradition and under-the-table payments. The upstart Southeastern and Southwestern Conferences had gotten too many of the best players and won too many games through scholarship enticements. Going forward, it would take money both above and below the NCAA table to recruit the best teams.

Chapter Twenty-Two:
The NCAA becomes fully Operational

When the NCAA was founded, its sole purpose was to ensure the safety and fairness of the game. Over the years, the NCAA has grown to regulate much more than just safety. It regulates school mascots, team names, recruiting, and eligibility guidelines as well as the actual rules on the field of play. Despite their non-profit status, they operate as a for-profit corporation and seek to continually grow their revenue and power.

In 1951, the NCAA hired a young college dropout named Walter Byers as Executive Director. He was a short fellow who "needed to be looked up to." It was a new position for the organization and there were hopes that somehow the NCAA could get control of college athletics. He was a twenty-nine year-old former journalist who would control the NCAA over the next thirty-six years and grow it from an annual convention boondoggle and tournament host into the dominant power in college athletics.

In college, Byers walked on to Rice University in the attempt to play football himself. The head coach at Rice was former SMU All-American Jimmy Kitts. He told the 5'- 6" Byers that he was too small and that he should just go home. Byers left Rice and transferred to the University of Iowa where he majored in journalism and then dropped out nine hours short of graduation to enroll in the U.S. Army. He was discharged for an eye problem and moved around the Northeast for a few years until he decided to give up journalism and go back home to the mid-west. There, he took a job as public relations assistant to the Big Ten Commissioner who was also the NCAA Secretary-Treasurer. Four years later he was offered the job as Executive Director of the NCAA, largely because nobody else wanted it.

In his new job, Byers discovered he had no office, no staff, no funding, and no authority. He did have the support of a number of schools that recognized the need for a functioning body. It was a good time for the NCAA to make a move because one thing Byers did have was a national scandal. The University of Kentucky basketball program was embroiled in a point shaving scandal that had gone national with pictures of players and gangsters making the papers everywhere.

Kentucky won the 1951 National Championship and was expected to defend it well in 1952. Byers convened an informal "Infractions Board" to set penalties against Kentucky but he knew it had no legitimacy. So, he lobbied Kentucky's conference opponents as well as administrators of Kentucky itself to accept the penalties. The NCAA Infractions Board had no actual authority to impose their penalties but made the argument that they were necessary to restore the public's faith in college sports. The scandal was serious enough and sufficient pressure was put on Kentucky, so that they finally accepted the penalty. Their basketball team was suspended and could not play for the 1952-53 season. Walter Byers had just bluffed his way into establishing a precedent that the weak and toothless NCAA actually had the command and institutional support to regulate college sports.

Fresh from his victory slamming Kentucky basketball with a version of the Death Penalty, Walter Byers knew that his organization lacked real power and enforcement ability. He sat down and re-examined the last attempt at setting up an enforcement mechanism, the 1948 Sanity Code. The NCAA did their job and found violators of the Code prohibiting athletic scholarships. They had detailed evidence on seven member institutions who continued to grant athletic scholarships after it had passed. The schools were called the "Sinful Seven." The rules were clear. The punishment required under the bylaws was expulsion from the NCAA. When Byers presented his case to the general membership to vote on expulsion, it wasn't even close. 60 for expulsion, 130 against. The vote rendered the NCAA enforcement regime toothless and insignificant. Byers realized that he had to find a way to get the member institutions to agree to punish other member institutions; otherwise any ideas of enforcement would just be more wasted effort.

To enforce the growing number of rules and to reassure the public that the NCAA was taking violations seriously, in 1953 the NCAA Council was given more enforcement powers it needed to be effective. First, it could impose sanctions without the approval of a majority of delegates. Second, the sanctions included a wide range of options, not just expulsion. The Council could ban a school from post-season play, limit television appearances, limit regular season contests to schools in their own conference, restrict the number of allowable recruiting visits, and reduce the number of students offered scholarships.

In 1955, Byers came up with the idea of having the presidents of member institutions sign a statement pledging to abide by NCAA rules and regulations. This was a good next step but Byers knew that if he punished the big universities too hard, even when caught cheating red-handed, he would risk losing all that he had gained. Byers had to go slowly, amass his power gradually.

As the years rolled by, the NCAA started to take action against violators. The low hanging fruit was collected first to make sure no member institutions revolted. Eventually, people began to pay attention to the NCAA and their newfound power. According to former PAC-Ten Commissioner Wiles Hallock, "Byers built the power of the NCAA on enforcement. Before enforcement, it didn't have any power; it was just a scheduling organization."

Byers also knew that the member schools were too diverse to agree on any course of action. He took advantage of it. The NCAA was made up of big schools, small schools, rich schools, and poor schools. All were expected to follow the same rules. As a result, there was no way to get a consensus from a majority on what rules meant and what punishments should be. Byers exploited this. When a member institution was facing an investigation, Byers and his staff maintained that they were simply following rules established by the members and agreed to by the university presidents. But in actuality, Byers was interpreting the rules however he wanted and enforcing only the ones that he chose to. There was no consensus to stop him.

Once Byers established a bit of power after successfully penalizing the Kentucky Basketball program, he needed to back it up with an independent funding source or he risked being shut down. The main athletic revenue stream at that time was ticket sales. But there was another intriguing source of income on the horizon, television.

Most schools feared a reduction in ticket sales if games were televised. Byers floated the idea of rotating games around the country each week so a specific school could receive wide exposure without suffering the weekly loss of too many ticket sales. The universities would get the lion's share of the money. All Byers wanted was a 12% cut of the contract. And he wanted one other thing; he wanted the money to flow through the NCAA first to make sure he got that cut.

Byers strapped on the strongest weapon in his arsenal: the NCAA as the only national representative of college football. In 1952, Byers approached the networks and cut a deal to televise all intercollegiate football. It was valued at $1.14

million dollars. Penn State and Notre Dame resisted as they had their own TV contracts. But when Byers threatened them with sanctions for not following NCAA bylaws, they folded.

With that first television contract, the NCAA achieved real power. They had the support of influential university presidents, they had the support of the public to enforce a "clean" game, and now they had an independent funding source. Walter Byers and the NCAA had arrived.

Chapter Twenty-Three:
SMU History

Southern Methodist University was chartered by the Methodist Episcopal Church in 1911. It took another four years to get Dallas Hall built, chiefly due to the city of Dallas' attempts to entice another college to the area. Classes started in the fall of 1915. On September 14, 1915 Coach Ray Morrison held his first practice, thus marking the birth of the SMU football program.

Morrison came to the school in June as the coach of the university's football, basketball, baseball, and track teams as well as an instructor of mathematics. A former All-Southern quarterback at Vanderbilt and a College Football Hall of Fame member, Morrison immediately installed the passing game at SMU. He composed SMU's first football team using mostly theology students which caused a local sportswriter to give them the nickname "The Parsons."

The SMU football team struggled under Morrison for the first three years before joining the Southwest Conference in 1918; then they struggled for two more years with losing records every year. In 1922 Morrison guided SMU to the first of ten straight winning seasons with a passing offense sportswriters referred to as "the Aerial Circus." At the time, most teams threw the ball five or six times per game. SMU threw thirty to forty times per game. With this style of offense, SMU posted a perfect 9-0 mark in 1923 and won the Southwest Conference title.

With winning came benefits and more fans. In 1926 SMU's Ownby Stadium was built on campus and named after an important booster Jordan C. Ownby. For the rest of the 1920's and throughout the 1930's, SMU's football program continued to rise. In 1935, undefeated SMU beat undefeated TCU and their All-American quarterback Sammy Baugh to win the National Championship title and a trip to the Rose Bowl. SMU travelled to Pasadena by train and partied all the way. An unserious SMU faced heavy underdog Stanford. Stanford scored the only touchdown winning 7-0 giving SMU a 12-1 record. The money earned at the Rose Bowl allowed SMU to pay off their ten-year debt on Ownby Stadium and narrowly prevented its foreclosure.

SMU entered the 1940's as a well-respected program becoming co-champions of the Southwest Conference in 1940. Through World War II the program suffered like most programs due to a lack of men. Then, after six consecutive losing seasons 1947 brought new excitement in the form of running back Doak Walker. He was the only three time All-American in SMU history and he won the Heisman Trophy in 1948. He also led SMU to SWC championships and Cotton Bowl invitations in both 1947 and 1948.

Over the course of his SMU career, Doak rushed for almost 2,000 yards, passed for over 1,600 yards, scored 288 points, kicked field goals and extra points, and averaged just under 40 yards per punt. He still leads SMU in all-time punt return yards at 750. The Mustangs had to move from Ownby Stadium to the Cotton Bowl to accommodate the large influx of fans that insisted on watching him play. That stadium became known as "The House that Doak built." Today the "Doak Walker Award" is given to the nation's best running back and is one of the highest honors in college football.

Playing with Doak for two seasons was Kyle Rote. Rote picked up where Walker left off and created his own legacy in a historic game against Notre Dame. Rote single handedly ran for 115 yards, threw for 146 yards, and scored all three of SMU touchdowns in a losing effort to Notre Dame. Undefeated Notre Dame went on to the National Championship that year with SMU being their only real scare. Rote's performance in that game was voted by the Texas Sportswriters Association as "The Outstanding Individual Performance by a Texas Athlete in the First Half of the 20th Century." Incredibly twenty-five years later, Notre Dame made Rote an "Honorary Member" to their championship team. After his senior year, Rote was runner-up for the Heisman Trophy and the first pick in the 1951 NFL draft.

In 1951 and 1956 SMU beat Notre Dame in aerial displays that caused even President Eisenhower to notice. He later commented that "an atheist is a guy who watches the Notre Dame-SMU game and doesn't care who wins." That quote was also attributed to comedian Bob Hope who was another fan and enjoyed the excitement of SMU football.

Throughout the 1950's new players arrived to lead SMU but we struggled to match our earlier successes. Forrest Gregg was voted to the Pro Football Hall of Fame and Vince Lombardi stated in his book *Run to Daylight* that Gregg was "the finest player I ever coached." Raymond Berry, an outstanding wide receiver, was also inducted into the Pro Football Hall of Fame after twelve years in the NFL.

Lamar Hunt, son of oil tycoon H.L. Hunt, played SMU football and was an avid sports enthusiast. In August 1959 he founded the American Football League (AFL) with the goal of bringing professional football to Texas. He started the Dallas Texans but had to compete with the newly formed Dallas Cowboys of the National Football league (NFL). In 1963 the Texans moved to Kansas City and became the Chiefs. The AFL and NFL merged in 1966 and Hunt proposed a championship game between them to be called "the

Super Bowl." Each year the winner of the AFC (AFL) is presented the "Lamar Hunt Trophy" in his honor.

Two time All-American "Dandy" Don Meredith played in the late 1950's. He was so popular on campus that students jokingly referred to SMU as Southern "Meredith" University. During his sophomore season, SMU installed an early version of the Run-and-Shoot offense with a spread formation using multiple wide receivers on each side. His .610 career completion percentage is the greatest of any passer in Mustang history but his defining attribute was his running ability which increased the pressure on opposing defenses. He later played for the Dallas Cowboys and hosted Monday Night Football on ABC.

From 1949 to 1960, twenty-six SMU players were drafted by the NFL, more than OU (22) and Texas (17), but we couldn't win the conference.

In the 1960's SMU introduced a new coach Hayden Fry, who was able to get SMU back into the national spotlight. In 1966 with a new version of the "Aerial Circus" under quarterback Chuck Hixson, SMU won the SWC for the first time in eighteen years and finished #9 in the nation. His main target was 5'8" Jerry LeVias the first black football player in the SWC. Hixson and LeVias continued their success in 1968 and led the 8-3 Mustangs to a dramatic win in the Bluebonnet Bowl over Oklahoma and a final ranking of #14.

LeVias had been deemed too small by many schools but Coach Fry saw in him the character, academic potential and skill that would be needed to successfully integrate the Southwest Conference. Once LeVias demonstrated his ability, Darrell Royal, head coach at Texas, quipped that LeVias "no longer looked too small." Texas passed over LeVias not only due to his size but because Texas would not begin to integrate until five years after SMU in 1970.

LeVias suffered the same kinds of hateful treatment Jackie Robinson had in integrating major league baseball in 1947. Opponents regularly taunted and sought to hurt him.

Some officials were biased against him, some fans screamed racial abuse, and there were countless mean-spirited letters and phone calls. He received a death threat serious enough to warrant law enforcement officers to be on the lookout for snipers.

The mistreatment continued throughout LeVias' career at SMU. At Baylor in 1967, a cheap shot resulted in profuse bleeding and an injury of his eye socket that later required surgery. No penalty was called. In his senior year, the Mustangs were in Fort Worth to play TCU. LeVias caught nine passes in a game that was tied midway through the fourth quarter when a TCU player knocked him to the ground, uttered a racial epithet, and spat in his face. LeVias took himself out of the game, threw his helmet down and announced loudly, "I quit!" Coach Fry came over to console an angry, miserable, crying LeVias on the bench. He agreed to go back in for the next punt return but said, "Coach, I'm going to run it back for a touchdown." LeVias caught the punt at his 11-yard line, headed up the middle, veered right and crossed back to the left while dodging would-be tacklers, cut into the open and outran everybody for an 89-yard touchdown that won the game.

LeVias went on to play six years in the NFL. He knew the significance of what he did in integrating the SWC, but during a symposium at Texas A&M-Galveston in 2002, when asked if he would do it all over again, his response was a succinct "no."

Throughout the 1960's, SMU struggled on the field except for those 1966 and 1968 seasons. Then enthusiasm and attendance began to drop as the Dallas Cowboys started taking football fans with no reason for an SMU affiliation away to Texas Stadium.

In the early 1970's, four different teams won the SWC and SMU wasn't one of them. But in 1976, SMU began a push for greatness again when Coach Ron Meyer was hired.

He was given the responsibility of reestablishing a championship reign on the SMU Hilltop.

Chapter Twenty-Four:
SMU Investigations

I kept hearing about how SMU was the most investigated and penalized school in NCAA history. The media kept repeating it so it had to be true. But I was confused. I was there and I didn't see much. I had lots of friends that played football. We shared stories about recruiting, and our recruiting trips were all pretty much the same. Meet the coaches, tour the facilities, go out to dinner, and hit a few parties to see what the co-eds looked like. There were meals paid for, T-shirts and hats given out, sometimes a few extra bucks spent beyond the $25 NCAA allowance, but it was all pretty trivial stuff. Maybe I didn't see all the cheating because I was a lineman and not a skilled player. That didn't fly either. Most of my friends were the skilled players and it was the same with them. But there had to be something. The NCAA said we were the most investigated and the most corrupt football program ever. I decided to verify that for myself.

The first NCAA investigation of SMU occurred in April 1958. The head coach was Bill Meek and the president of the school was Willis M. Tate. The previous two seasons, SMU went 4-6 in 1956 and beat Texas 20-19, and then 4-5 in 1957 and beat Texas again 19-12. The Mustangs had not been dominating the Southwest Conference but they had been beating Texas. There was no media investigation or SMU athlete that began this investigation. SMU was accused by another school within the Southwest Conference.

The violation alleged was that a football booster arranged and provided an SMU recruit with a summer job in the oil patch. The investigator found that the recruit actually did do the job, and that the pay was commensurate with the responsibilities. However, the conclusion of the NCAA was that the recruit did not have sufficient experience to perform the job prior to doing it. After all, what young person hires on to a job with no experience? The NCAA ruled that the job was created specifically for the recruit and was therefore a violation. SMU was put on probation with no other penalties for a period of one year. It was pretty thin stuff. Maybe the next investigation would be more serious.

The second NCAA investigation of SMU occurred seven years later in April 1965. There was a different head coach, Hayden Fry, and the school president was still Willis M. Tate. SMU's football team went 2–8 in 1962 and 4–6 in 1963. Apparently, two enrolled student-athletes didn't have the money to go home for Christmas. The NCAA found that over the holidays, SMU provided free transportation to the two student-athletes from the university's campus to their homes and then returned them to campus. The NCAA made special note of the cooperation that the Southwest Conference and SMU in particular gave to the NCAA in resolving this case. SMU was put on two years' probation and banned from postseason play and TV for two years. These violations were also pretty thin but the penalties sure weren't. I remembered reading about this probation and how mad Coach Fry was at UT. He was convinced they turned us in so he turned them in for something similar. Things were already getting ridiculous.

The third NCAA investigation occurred ten years later in August 1974. The new head coach was Dave Smith and the new president was Dr. Paul Hardin. SMU's football team went 7–4 in 1972 and 6–3 in 1973. President Hardin learned in 1972 that Coach Fry bought dinner for a few players and their dates in recognition of outstanding plays. He quietly got rid of Fry. Then in 1974, he learned that Coach Smith was paying players small amounts of cash for outstanding plays in practice and in games. He also learned that Smith gave players cash in lieu of their two customary game tickets, occasionally gave players movie passes, and he gave a recruit some pocket money and tickets to a Cowboy game. Twenty-three players were found to have received cash from Coach Smith and were declared ineligible. Later, all twenty-three players had their eligibility restored. SMU self-disclosed all the infractions as President Hardin had been encouraged to do at NCAA conventions.

The NCAA stated that "The Committee on Infractions believes the actions taken by the president of the university are highly commendable, the University's self-disclosure of these violations and the resultant disciplinary actions were considered by the committee to be mitigating factors in the determination of the penalties imposed by the NCAA." SMU was placed on two years' probation, prevented from appearing on television during those two years, and prohibited from postseason play. SMU went even further than the NCAA and decided that since Coach Smith was directly involved, they would replace his four-year contract with a one-year contract and put him on one-year school probation. It sounded to me like the NCAA didn't mitigate anything and that the penalties were excessive.

President Hardin fought with the SMU Board of Governors about many things but after firing popular Head Coach Hayden Fry and then self-disclosing the infractions to the NCAA that resulted in the 1974 probation, he was asked to resign by the Board.

The fourth NCAA investigation occurred after Smith met the terms of the school probation in January 1975 and SMU signed him to a new contract. David Berst, the NCAA's Director of Enforcement, was upset and said "as far as the

NCAA was concerned Smith was on a form of probation forever. Normally, the probation period of the coach runs concurrently with the school's probation." He interpreted SMU's awarding Smith a new contract as a "slap in the face" and was "stomping on the desk" he was so mad. He told his investigator to "zero in" on SMU Assistant Coach Julius Glosson because "he was a black coach recruiting ghetto athletes." The investigator assigned was quoted as saying "give me six weeks and I could put any school in the country on probation." Nothing serious was dug up, but Berst was able to put together enough of a case.

They found that Glosson bought South Oak Cliff quarterback Rod Gerald and his girlfriend lunch, that he gave the recruit a ride home, and that he gave him small amounts of cash. The total transaction was $25. When asked if he broke any NCAA rules, Glosson replied "No." But that was enough for a school already on probation. The sanctions included extending the 1974-76 probation for an additional year through 1977 and SMU had to permanently disassociate itself from Coach Glosson.

SMU got the message, fired Coach Smith, and told the new head coach he could keep any coach from Smith's staff except Glosson. Julius Glosson had been responsible for roaming the black neighborhoods of Dallas and convincing top players to come to SMU when there were no blacks in the SWC and only a few at SMU. He sold SMU's ability to provide "a first rate education" and bragged of his ability to recruit blacks to come to a school with a country club reputation. Even after being let go, Glosson never spoke poorly of SMU or his time coaching there.

But he was collateral damage in Berst's quest to get SMU. Essentially blackballed from coaching by the NCAA, Glosson was sent back to the poor part of town to try and eke out a living. In the middle of a recession, he focused on trying to put food on the table for his family. The only work he found was a series of menial jobs including the graveyard shift on a loading dock. In 1983 he was shot to death at the age of forty-one. The NCAA did make note of his passing in their newsletter though.

When looking at all the violations, they were minor and unrelated. In a weird way I wished I had found more. After all that I heard about how bad we were, it was disappointing. Coaches gave a few rides or some pocket money to a few players. Some meals or movie tickets were provided. Coaches who provided the benefits were disassociated or were not at SMU over long enough time periods to establish a pattern of abuse. Nonetheless, from 1958 through 1977, SMU had now been placed on probation a total of four times. It didn't matter how trivial, or how many years had elapsed, or whether there were four different coaches and three different school presidents. The NCAA was building a case that SMU was a repeat violator.

I think a big part of the NCAA's animosity towards SMU was the firing of President Hardin in 1974. At the time, there was a nationwide push to get "institutional control" over athletics. Since college football's founding, teams had operated outside the direct control of schools and their presidents. They had separate fundraising, separate budgets, and separate staffs. This made it very difficult for the NCAA which was made up of school presidents, to get control. For SMU to fire our president mainly because he was following NCAA policy and trying to exert his control over athletics must have caused Berst and his boss Walter Byers considerable problems.

President Hardin later told the New York Post that "at least six Southwest Conference presidents confessed that they could not have turned in their schools as he had done." I'm sure that event more than any other, pissed off the NCAA and set us up for continued pursuit by their enforcement division. We set back their efforts at gaining institutional control over athletics, and we would not be forgotten.

Chapter Twenty-Five:
Coach Ron Meyer

Throughout the late 1960's and through the 1970's, the Southwest Conference was largely the University of Texas Conference. They won the conference in 1968, 1969, 1970, 1971, 1972, 1973, 1975, and 1977. The only other team during this era that was consistently competitive was Arkansas. SMU had a great history but we had been languishing in the middle of the Southwest Conference for years. In 1966 SMU made a slight comeback by winning the Southwest Conference for the first time since 1948. In 1968 quarterback Chuck Hixson and wide receiver Jerry LeVias combined to help SMU to its first bowl victory since the Doak Walker 1949 Cotton Bowl win. But that was it. Those two moments cast a light dusting of glory over what was a long and difficult dry spell.

In January 1976, after firing Coach Dave Smith, SMU decided to get serious. We hired Coach Ron Meyer. He was thirty-five, he was handsome, he was personable, and he was poor. The son of a truck driver, he walked on to the football team at Purdue and earned a starting position through ambition and hard work. He ended up as an assistant coach there. Then he was a scout for the Dallas Cowboys in 1971-72 where he got the Super Bowl ring he wore so visibly. After the Cowboys, he successfully turned around the football program at small time UNLV accumulating a 27-8 record over three years. He pursued the head coaching job at SMU after others turned it down and he was exactly what the fading glory of a tired SMU craved.

Ron Meyer was flashy. He knew he was destined to be a great coach and he acted like it. When it came to coaching and recruiting, nobody was going to out hustle him. He saw the former greatness of SMU and vowed to rebuild it. He was a man on a mission. SMU saw in him a young aggressive builder and gave him a long term five-year contract to give him enough time to get the job done.

His first recruiting class was not what he had in mind. With only a few weeks to recruit, it was small. He inked just nine players on signing day. Still, he managed to sign some legitimate blue chippers including future All-American Emanuel Tolbert. The first thing he did on the field was take control of a lackluster team that went 4-7 in 1975 by adopting the hard core military style training that worked for him at UNLV. He instituted "Mustang Reminders" if a player was late or missed a meeting (100 yards running and dropping chest first to the ground every 5 yards). Even though Meyer was gone by the time I got there in 1984, he left the Reminders behind and I cursed that man more than a few times.

His 1976 season was worse at 3-8 than former coach Dave Smith's last season. This was certainly not what SMU hoped. When signing day rolled around in February 1977, Meyer's nets were full with a class of twenty-eight. His ability to recruit players such as Mike Ford, a highly-touted quarterback from Mesquite High School helped build the foundation for "Mustang Mania." While the incoming freshmen looked good, they only translated into one more win over the previous year as SMU finished 4-7.

The 1978 recruiting class was a huge step up. Out of nowhere Ron Meyer outhustled and outworked everyone in the SWC to sign the 10th best class in the country. That season, Ford became the nation's second-ranked passer and threw for 3,007 yards. His main target was Tolbert, an All-American with blazing speed.

In a three game road trip, SMU signaled they were back. They knocked off Florida in Gainesville, narrowly lost to #4 Penn State making the Nittany Lions have to come from behind to win, and then tied heavily favored Ohio State just missing a last second winning field goal. The 1978 season may have only been 4-6-1, but SMU played a tough schedule and three of our losses were by less than a touchdown. With twenty-four freshmen on our sixty-man traveling squad SMU was young, but we were starting to play better.

In 1979 Mustang Mania was taking root and ushered in a new era for SMU football: the Mustangs began playing all of their home games at Texas Stadium. Accompanying the move was a freshman class which lifted SMU football to new heights. Meyer brought in the greatest recruiting class SMU had ever seen. Ranked #3 in the country behind USC and Notre Dame, that class put SMU football on the map. The biggest recruits were Craig James and Eric Dickerson, but the entire class was made up of future NFL greats. Dickerson had committed to Texas A&M and received a gold Pontiac Trans-Am the next day. But he changed his mind and kept the car. The shocked Aggies could only watch as he drove his new car to Dallas to attend SMU. Dickerson said his grandmother put down approximately $5,000 and agreed to make the $200 payments if he would stay in Texas to go to college. An NCAA investigator looked into it and said "everything looked clean."

Meyer promised Dickerson and James that they would play together as split backs in the wishbone or the veer. Their freshman year James played well gaining 761 yards but Dickerson struggled with hamstring pulls, thigh bruises, a concussion, and turf toe. He missed two games, ran for only 477 yards, and thought of transferring. The Mustangs finished 1979 at 5-6, however, Eric Dickerson and Craig James combined that year to rush for 1,239 yards and the "Pony Express" was born.

Under Athletic Director Russ Potts, donations to the SMU Mustang Club increased from $150,000 to almost $3 million and Mustang Mania was filling Texas Stadium. The campaign targeted each resident of Dallas seven times per day during the football season. On the radio when you woke up, in your car as you drove to work, from a roadside billboard, on a passing bumper sticker, from pocket schedules on every secretary's desk, and on wall posters where you bought gas or had lunch. SMU promoted the spectacle not the contest.

As an example, the 1979 SMU v. Baylor was a dog of a game. Neither had a chance in the SWC and it was being played the same day as the Texas v. OU game. SMU billed the game as the Baptists v. the Methodists, gave out 30,000 tickets to churches and resulted in 66,000 fans for a 65,000 capacity stadium. It was embarrassing that they didn't have the room, but it was a sellout for the game. And according to Potts, "sellouts breed sellouts."

While Meyer continued bringing in top recruit after top recruit, word on the street grew. He was too flashy, too successful and fast for the other Southwest Conference head coaches and recruiters. He was an outsider who cheated "too much." There was "normal" cheating and then there was Ron Meyer style cheating. He broke too many of the "rules." He was a machine and worked too late and too hard. He signed too many blue chip athletes and disregarded too many of the NCAA regulations that he disagreed with. The other SWC coaches could not stand him. He made them look bad. Something would have to be done about this guy.

Chapter Twenty-Six:
1980 - The Jump

As is usually the case, top recruits eventually translate into winning seasons. It took a few years, but by 1980 the Mustangs were ready and made the jump. Eric Dickerson and Craig James gave the Mustangs one of the nation's top backfield duos and QB Mike Ford returned to the team after a knee injury limited him to just two starts in 1979. Leading the defense were future All-Americans John Simmons and Harvey Armstrong.

SMU started 4-0 before losing two in a row to Baylor and Houston mainly due to turnovers. Meyer tried the wishbone, the veer, and every other combination to work his two star tailbacks. He ran a multiple offense and threw around thirty times a game under Ford. After the Houston game, Meyer decided to change to a ball control attack under an I-formation against the #2 ranked Texas Longhorns. He replaced Ford with the smaller and quicker freshman Lance McIlhenny and started running the option. SMU upset Texas 20-6 knocking them off their national championship pace.

It was SMU's first victory over Texas since 1966 and it was noticed. Several days after the Texas win in one of those huge coincidences that seemed to keep popping up, the

NCAA notified SMU that they were opening a "Preliminary Inquiry" into our recruiting practices.

SMU had four games left in the season. We decided to stick with the option, to throw the ball only ten times a game, and to rotate our two tailbacks in rather than playing them at the same time. SMU finished the regular season 8-3 ranked #19. We met the 11-1 BYU Cougars ranked #14 under QB Jim McMahon in the Holiday Bowl. It was SMU's first bowl appearance since a 1968 win over Oklahoma in the Bluebonnet Bowl. SMU led 45-25 with four minutes to play when McMahon orchestrated the greatest comeback I had ever seen.

BYU scored, recovered an onside kick and scored again. With time running out, McMahon threw two incomplete passes in the end zone before completing his third attempted Hail Mary for the tying score. The PAT gave the game to BYU with no time left on the clock.

Even though I was a McMahon fan, I was introduced to the SMU Mustangs in that game. I saw an exciting offense with Eric Dickerson, Craig James, and Lance McIlhenny. I saw their cool uniforms and their flamboyant coach. They were very different from the plodding offenses of the Big Eight and the lesser teams of the WAC. I could get excited about playing for such a team.

SMU may have been disappointed by the BYU loss but it was a good season. The Mustangs finished with an 8-4 record and the school's first national ranking (20th) since 1968. Average attendance at home games previously averaged 26,000 but skyrocketed to over 52,000 that year with 90% of the undergraduate student body attending each home game. The 1980 season was the breakout season we had worked for. SMU had figured out how to use our twin tailbacks and looked forward to a full 1981 season running the option and the *Pony Express*.

The NCAA had other plans for us. They sent and released an official Letter of Inquiry on February 11, 1981, the same day as National Signing Day. It was a coincidence that they chose that day to release the letter. To no one's surprise, we did not sign a ranked class that year.

In the Letter of Inquiry were numerous allegations from players who had gone to other schools in the SWC. The investigation was a collective one as the entire conference combined to knock us down. There was little wonder who turned us in. Various accounts named Baylor, TCU, Texas and Arkansas, but surely the rest of the SWC teams silently applauded. Every team competed for the same recruits and we all struggled for primacy. The animosity within the conference was becoming so great that rivals were becoming enemies. Ron Meyer was the outsider who broke the good 'ol boy rules on recruiting and then he had the temerity to start winning with those recruits.

The NCAA concluded their investigation four months later and announced a two-year probation for the 1981 and 1982 seasons including a one-year ban on television appearances and postseason bowls for the 1981 football season.

The violations cited were: the head coach led recruits to believe that they were allowed to sell their complementary game tickets for more than face value, a recruit's uncle was allowed to stay at a booster's house and use his car, a booster bought a meal for two recruits and gave them tickets to a game and a ride. Various recruits were contacted too many times at their schools and at home, and an assistant coach gave allowed entertainment money directly to recruits instead of their hosts. The NCAA also discovered that recruits were given pictures of themselves on campus and a coach played racquetball with one of them on a recruiting trip.

While these allegations were minor in nature, they were all the NCAA could dig up. It was another coincidence that all the infractions involved recruits that attended other schools and not SMU. The recruits interviewed were mainly players who signed with Texas and were gathered by Texas officials and provided to the NCAA. The driving factor in the

NCAA's sanctions referenced the number of times we had been investigated...not the seriousness of the violations.

According to the NCAA: "In reviewing this matter, the committee was particularly concerned that this case represents the third time in the last seven years that the Southern Methodist University football program has been found to be in violation of significant NCAA rules," said Charles Alan Wright, University of Texas Professor, Texas football booster, and Chair of the NCAA Committee on Infractions. "Although the committee recognizes the current president, director of athletics, and head football coach were not associated with the institution at the time previous cases were considered, the committee is required to take into account past violations."

In a pattern that would repeat, the University of Texas kept popping up and we kept getting penalized for being investigated rather than for actual violations. The NCAA was sure SMU had broken more rules; they just couldn't prove it. They believed SMU had gotten so good so fast that we just had to be cheating. So the NCAA wrote up what they could as a way of knocking us back down. More than that they put us on notice and signaled that they were watching us. The NCAA may have closed down this case, but they most definitely did not close down their investigation.

The 1981 Mustangs could not play on television and we were ineligible for postseason bowl games, but we could still go undefeated and claim a conference and possibly even a national championship. SMU took off with a 6-0 start. Our offense was predictable but unstoppable. 82% of the time McIlhenny pitched the ball to either James or Dickerson. Together, these two backs rotated in every other series, averaged 46 carries, and yet remained rested throughout the game. SMU also ran two offensive lines and rotated them in too, so our entire offense could keep pounding you with fresh linemen and fresh tailbacks for four full quarters.

Game seven was against Texas. Texas was 4-1 (lost to Arkansas the week before) and ranked #10 in the country when they came to Dallas to play the #8 ranked Mustangs. Texas won in a defensive battle 9 - 7 avenging their loss in 1980. SMU would go on to win our remaining games and finished the season 10-1 with a final ranking of #5.

Even though SMU lost to Texas, we had the best record in the Southwest Conference and were crowned champions for the first time since 1966. Unable to accept our earned Cotton Bowl invitation, SMU had to sit out that bowl season and watched Texas, as SWC runner-up, play in our stead. In 1982, that would not happen.

Chapter Twenty-Seven:
Coach Bobby Collins

1982 was supposed to be payback for Texas turning us in and the NCAA for shutting us out. We were still on probation, but this year we could play on TV and we could play in a postseason bowl game.

After leading the Mustangs to an 11-1 record and SWC Championship in 1981, the following January Coach Ron Meyer abruptly left SMU to coach the New England Patriots. It had always been his goal to be an NFL coach, but it was bad timing for us.

SMU felt that we had rebuilt our program to such a degree that we could have our pick of several great coaches to replace him. Unfortunately, SMU didn't have enough time. Meyer quit the month before National Signing Day without leaving a committed recruiting class. It was similar to the circumstances Meyer faced when he came to SMU in 1976. Our new coach would have to work fast to salvage a 1982 class. The successful recruiting classes of the late 70's were rotating through. It was imperative that the momentum Meyer built be maintained.

Athletic Director Bob Hitch promised to replace Meyer within three days. He thought he could sell the national prominence SMU had achieved along with a returning team that would compete for the national championship but he was turned down by his first three choices.

It was a rush and unrealistic to think a top tier coach could make a decision that fast. But Coach Bobby Collins of Southern Mississippi was different. He was arguably a top tier coach, but better than that he was a long term personal friend of Hitch's. Hitch called in a favor, which Thurman "Bobby" Collins Jr. accepted on Monday January 18, 1982. Per Hitch's commitment, Collins became SMU's newest head football coach just three days after Meyer left.

Collins began his college career as quarterback at Mississippi State and was team captain in 1954 under Head Coach Darrell Royal who would later achieve fame at Texas. He toiled as an assistant coach for almost twenty years before Southern Mississippi offered him the head coaching position in 1975. Over the next seven years, he built that regional school into a national power and took them to two bowl games in his last two years.

Despite his credentials, he was an awkward fit for Big "D." Dallas and SMU were big city and big time and Collins was more small town. Hitch had talked him into it and Collins didn't really have enough time to evaluate our program. It was a significant step up for him and his initial goal was to simply not screw up the machine that Meyer and SMU had built. Over his five-year tenure, he met that goal and more. Collins would become the winningest coach in SMU history (43-14-1) and from 1982-1984 the winningest coach in America (31-4-1).

Our returning backfield of Dickerson and James had finished #4 in the nation in rushing. The entire offense was two deep and the defense led the nation in interceptions while allowing only 12.5 points per game. We were picked pre-season #4 and favored to win the SWC again. But this time, free from NCAA sanctions we were picked to play in the Cotton Bowl, and win it.

Collins' first season in 1982 began where Meyer's had left off in 1981. SMU quickly won the first six games only struggling against TCU (16-13) and Baylor (22-19). Ranked #5, we met #19 Texas October 23. Texas was the only team that had beaten us in 1981. This year we were favored again and they looked to knock us off...again. They planned to control the ball and keep the ball from Dickerson and James. Our tailbacks were averaging 280.6 yards per game and Texas planned to hurt them. Their goal was to use Texas style intimidation and tradition at home in Austin to rattle us. Texas players were interviewed trashing our runners saying how we were "crybabies" that we "couldn't take a lick" and how they were going to make "fierce tackles." The idea was to psyche us out. The Mustang players read all the stories and laughed it off. "What, do they think we're freshmen?" said Dickerson.

SMU went on to beat Texas 30-17 and extended our winning streak to eleven, the longest in the nation. Three more lopsided wins against Texas A&M, Rice, and Texas Tech set up a showdown between the undefeated and #2 ranked Mustangs against the 8-1 and #9 ranked Arkansas Razorbacks for the SWC Championship and rights to the Cotton Bowl.

Coach Collins had set his expectations for the team at the beginning of the season. The goals were to defend the conference championship and go to the Cotton Bowl. If we did that, it would be a successful season. He did not have a primary goal of winning a national championship and did not think the polls would break for SMU against the larger big time football schools. If it happened, great. But that was goal #3 after the SWC Championship and a Cotton Bowl Victory.

SMU was trailing 17-10 late in the game when we scored to make it 17-16 Arkansas. Collins went safely for the PAT, the tie, and the guaranteed SWC Championship over the riskier two-point conversion. If we converted we would have a better chance at the national championship. But if we

146

didn't convert we would have lost the conference, the Cotton Bowl berth, and the national championship. SMU hit the PAT for a 17-17 tie.

Collins confidently described his decision as an "easy call." He knew from previous experiences the only way a school like SMU would make a major bowl was to win the conference. Bowl committees did not want smaller private schools no matter what their national ranking. Therefore our only way in was to win the SWC for the guaranteed link to the Cotton Bowl.

In the 1983 Cotton Bowl #4 SMU met #6 Pittsburgh led by QB Dan Marino. Run oriented SWC teams like SMU were not used to the passing offense of Marino and Company. Likewise, the Pittsburgh defense was unfamiliar with SMU's option style offense. Pittsburgh looked to exploit their passing game by running four receivers to flood our half-man half-zone pass defense. It worked. Pitt was able to drive the ball and only a fumble at the SMU 2 prevented an early score. On defense, Pitt tried to push everything inside to prevent Dickerson and James from getting outside for yardage. They wanted to take away the pitch and force McIlhenny to have to keep the ball. Then, they planned to punish McIlhenny.

On SMU's initial drive Pitt was flagged for four penalties. Two were personal fouls as they tried to hack McIlhenny, a face mask, and then another personal foul. Pitt was trying to intimidate SMU on the field rather than in the newspapers like Texas attempted.

At the half neither SMU which averaged 31 points a game, nor Pitt which averaged 29 points a game, had scored. In the second, Pitt drove for a field goal to take a 3-0 lead. SMU answered and drove to the Pitt 11. McIlhenny optioned left to James for two yards. The next play he optioned right and the Pitt defenders went for James, but this time McIlhenny kept it and ran untouched for the score and the win. SMU 7 - Pitt 3. Nobody had held Pitt to three or less points since 1975.

11-0-1 SMU ended the season as the only undefeated school in the country and then lost a questionable final ranking to 11-1 Penn State for the National Championship. We came in second in voting, just like Collins predicted. The supposed reason? Our tie with #9 ranked Arkansas in the final regular season game. Meanwhile National Champion Penn State had lost to an Alabama team that was unranked with four losses.

A little more than one month after beating Pitt, Bobby Collins signed the 6th best class in the country. It was comparable to the great 1979 class. With this class, it was assured that SMU would dominate the SWC for the next four years.

Just days after signing that class our conference rivals passed on to the NCAA information about our recruiting practices again. This hearsay evidence was used to open another SMU investigation. Three weeks after receiving that information, the NCAA sent SMU a Preliminary Letter of Inquiry signifying the beginning of this new investigation. The NCAA could work fast when they wanted to.

The 1983 season was supposed to be a rebuilding year after the great 1979 class graduated and SMU had to coach up younger players. As such, the 1982 2nd ranked Mustangs began the 1983 season ranked only #19. We lost our starting Pony Express tailbacks and most of our defensive greats moved on to the NFL. Tailbacks Reggie Dupard and Jeff Atkins replaced Dickerson and James but our coaches were confident they would continue the tradition. Our young defense was fast and ranked 2nd in the country.

With an almost completely new team, we kept on rolling. We beat our first 5 opponents and worked our way up to 12th. As we neared mid-season against 4-0 and 2nd ranked Texas, it looked like a rematch of last year's battle except that this year, Texas was favored. With three minutes left in the game SMU scored to make it 13-12 Texas. Unlike last year's Arkansas tie, SMU went for the two point conversion and the win instead of a tying PAT. McIlhenny's pass to Dupard was short. Texas added a late safety to seal their victory 15-12 and ended our 21 game winning streak.

SMU won the rest of our regular season games to finish 10-1 and ranked 6th including a season ending rematch and shutout of Arkansas, its first shutout in 125 games.

That failed two point conversion against Texas cost us another SWC championship, another undefeated trip to the Cotton Bowl, and another shot at the national championship. We had gone 30-2-1 over the previous three seasons with both of our losses to Texas by a total of 5 points.

For all of our efforts and all of our successes, we were passed over by all four of the big bowls that we had a shot at (Orange, Sugar, Fiesta, and Cotton). Worse, 9 teams with lower rankings went to better bowls with bigger payouts than the Mustangs. Bobby Collins was right again. The only way into a major bowl for a school like SMU, was to win the conference. Second place, regardless of ranking, meant bowl snubs.

With no other option available, #6 SMU as the Southwest Conference runner up, went on to an unenthusiastic post season game in the El Paso, Texas Sun Bowl. There were only 16 bowl games in existence at the time, it was that or nothing. We played an unranked 7-4 Alabama team and played them poorly. Alabama promptly beat SMU 28-7 in what most everyone agrees was a let down to the season that could have been.

Our problem went beyond rankings and bowl status. We needed the big money that only came from a big bowl. There were no conference television contracts with big money at the time. It was ticket sales, television revenue, and bowl payouts. Back then, most colleges had to get into a major bowl or they would run a deficit. For a school like SMU, it was win the conference or lose money in football.

Most of the schools in the old SWC were in the same boat. Texas, Texas A&M, and Arkansas could reasonably expect to play on TV and get to a decent bowl without winning the conference. But SMU, TCU, Baylor, Texas Tech, Rice, and Houston had no chance unless they won it. To win meant getting the best recruits. To get the best recruits meant out bidding our rivals for them. In the SWC, the race was on.

Chapter Twenty-Eight:
The Trap

After the threat of the CFA and the attempted power grab by the President's Commission, it didn't take Walter Byers long to realize schools could think on their own and certainly organize without the help of the NCAA. Then the 1984 U.S. Supreme Court decision in favor of the CFA further damaged his authority and labeled his group criminals while cutting their funding.

With football television revenue dried up, the only remaining source of income for the NCAA was the *March Madness* Basketball Tournament. The tournament was 100% owned by the NCAA, and Byers got lucky. Thanks to cable television, basketball revenue began to grow at the exact same time the NCAA lost its football contracts. That increase at first covered and then exceeded the lost football revenue. But he had to protect that money. If anything happened to the basketball revenue stream, it would be the end of the NCAA. Byers needed something to prove the NCAA's importance and value to member universities.

The loss of football revenue rattled Byers but the loss of his authority rattled him more. He decided the NCAA needed to reassert that authority. If Byers had learned anything over the last thirty odd years it was that the most effective way to assert authority was to use it. His standard operating procedure had been to selectively pick schools to hammer depending on the message he wanted to send the other members. In the 1980's, Byers' message was that he and the NCAA were still in charge.

Enforcement had never been a priority within the NCAA. Their budget and minimal staffing reflected that neglect. "Cheating" had gone on from day one in college football and the proposition that cheating had gotten out of hand was not factual. Players had been consistently paid throughout college football history and the NCAA only responded to egregious cheating and to selected tips that they wanted to pursue. They never had enough staff to handle all the allegations sent in (according to David Berst they had 30-50 active files in a given year) and never tried to make the case for more resources to handle them all. But now the NCAA was desperate.

Enforcement was what gave the NCAA power. It was the one thing all schools could more or less agree on. The NCAA could not afford to be viewed as irrelevant or powerless and expect to survive. So enforcement was the tool Byers promoted to justify the NCAA's continued existence.

In 1984 the NCAA had successfully created outrage at the level of cheating across the country. Many schools besides SMU were trotted out as examples of cheaters. In a successful response to this effort, the NCAA was able to call a Special Convention where more specific and severe penalties were passed and the NCAA powers of enforcement were renewed. The NCAA needed to prove their relevance to the membership, and the membership needed somebody to clean up all the "cheating." It was perfect.

But *everybody* was cheating. More and more money was pouring into the game and more and more teams were willing to cut corners to get that money. The NCAA began a high profile selection of schools to investigate for recruiting violations. They targeted Oklahoma and Georgia of course

(Plaintiffs in the U.S. Supreme Court case), and then it reads as a who's who of college football: Auburn, ASU, SMU, Miami, UCLA, Oregon, Wisconsin, USC, Clemson, Arizona, North Carolina, Florida State, Florida, Illinois, and on and on it goes. I've read it was called the "Golden Age" of NCAA investigations. I think it was the reaction of a scared bureaucracy lashing out to prove its relevance and authority.

It didn't take the NCAA long to realize that if they kept chasing all the member schools, they would end up angering all the member schools. A better strategy was to target the same team over and over. They could raise the outrage against cheating while minimizing the outrage against the NCAA.

The formula for the NCAA to make this work was simple. There was a 1960's Radical named Saul Alinsky. He was famous for his book "Rules for Radicals" and his most famous quote was "pick a target, freeze it, personalize it, and then polarize it." The NCAA needed a target to freeze, personalize, and polarize.

There was no way the NCAA was going after one of the big boys. They needed somebody smaller, somebody that wouldn't have the political power to hit back, somebody that looked like they deserved it. They weren't specifically targeting SMU but we fit the profile.

We were small, elitist, and probably still cheating. We had a fractured conference where everyone turned each other in and hated each other. There was no risk the SWC would ride to our rescue. We were not part of the state college big time football club. We had fired our president who attempted to follow the NCAA rules and we had been investigated and penalized five times over the last thirty years. Yes, those investigations were unrelated and in most cases minor but that wouldn't matter. SMU was perfect.

The fall 1985 sanctions doomed us. The NCAA knew that they had not uncovered all of our violations. They knew they had merely scratched the surface, but they wrapped up

153

the investigation anyway. It didn't matter. The real strategy was to close down all the options for SMU to escape.

They wrote into the infractions report that "this investigation represented the most recent in a string of probations going back to 1956." They wrote that we "represented a habitual offender" and any further violations would be treated "even more severely." They penalized us a full recruiting class in 1986 and half the 1987 class for paying just one recruit.

They did not write into our infractions report the same verbiage they would write into Texas' 1986 report. In that report, Texas got all non-disclosed violations from their past erased. They got the chance to wind down their payment system without risk of further penalties. Texas wouldn't have to worry about a paid player coming forward and blackmailing them. We were not so fortunate.

The NCAA showed us with the TCU penalties what we could expect if our system was fully exposed. The message was clear. We could not voluntarily shut down our payment system and self-report to the NCAA. Nor could we stop paying the current players on the "payroll" for fear they would go public and also doom our program.

We were isolated within our conference. We had been successfully labeled in the media as a chronic cheater. We had been investigated a sufficient number of times for the NCAA to brand us a "repeat offender." We had been penalized severely without having disclosed all our violations.

The NCAA says "there are no undercover assignments" but now they would lie in wait. They had successfully boxed us in and had five long years to spring the trap. We had no way out and the NCAA knew it. It would just be a matter of time.

Chapter Twenty-Nine:
The Decision

We didn't know it yet but they had us. By August 1985, SMU was wedged so deep in the trap that there was no way to get out without triggering a real or a de facto Death Penalty. The NCAA was aware of our situation and did not allow us an escape hatch. It was in this context that SMU leadership had to make a decision.

The payment system set up under Ron Meyer had been dramatically wound down over the years. The 1983 recruiting class was the last significant use of the system to help get players. In the 1984 class there were paid recruits but few in comparison to previous classes. Sean Stopperich was the only one from that class discovered by the NCAA. With the open NCAA investigation and the difficulty in recruiting, the 1985 class was neither paid nor ranked. Due to the 1985 probation and elimination of scholarships, the 1986 class would consist of all walk-ons. The pressure the NCAA had put on SMU was working. The boosters were pushed out, our national stature was diminished, and the penalties were killing us.

There were no more payments for recruiting athletes. The only payments being made were to thirteen "hangover" student-athletes mainly from the 1983 class. The recruiting war over that class prompted the recent investigation and now their ongoing monthly stipends were the issue. The payments averaged $400 each and occurred only during the academic school year.

In mid-August 1985 SMU lost its NCAA appeal and accepted the sanctions. Athletes were coming back to campus and would soon be looking for those monthly stipends. Our president knew about the payment system and wanted it shut down. Selected members of the Board of Governors, Athletic Department, coaches, players, students, the NCAA, and the media, hell everybody knew, or at least had a reasonable suspicion that we still had players on the payroll. What nobody knew was what we were going to do after the September 1, 1985 effective start date for the Death Penalty.

It's easy for outsiders who have no understanding of the context to say we should have just shut it down; clearly it was the ethical thing to do. These same outsiders say that because we chose to not shut it down, and that the decision was made at the highest levels within SMU, it was even more heinous.

The truth was that the school leaders could feel the noose tightening and everybody at SMU wanted the payment system shut down, but nobody wanted to take responsibility for being the one to do it. We were in so deep that the only ways of getting out were potentially costly and damaging to the school. There were four options; none of them were good.

Option one was to shut down the payment program and then self-report the violations to the NCAA. This option would preempt the possibility of the system being exposed and would throw SMU on the mercy of the NCAA. TCU's self-reported violations and resulting penalties in 1986 demonstrated the kind of mercy the NCAA had in mind during those years. With SMU's track record, we could expect even less mercy. The advantage of this option is that it was the ethical decision and would have taken the Death Penalty sanction off the table as the payments would have stopped before the September 1 drop dead date.

156

Option two was to shut down the payment program and not self-report to the NCAA. The players receiving payments relied on that money for living expenses and to help with rent, groceries, gas, insurance, and other college costs. Those players had no resources from anyone to make up their shortfalls. From SMU's perspective, without that extra money, those players would be put in a desperate position. It was impossible to know what they might do. It was reasonable to assume that they could not have continued at SMU. They might have dropped out or exposed the payment system to the media or NCAA. SMU leaders would have expected no difference in NCAA penalties if we were exposed or if we self-disclosed.

Option three was to continue the payment program regardless of the risks. Previously, schools that were sanctioned for cheating kept right on cheating, including SMU. Earlier NCAA penalties were not that serious and did not threaten a school's ability to continue to play and win. But these new penalties changed the calculus. The ability to reduce scholarships, ban coaches and players, and terminate an entire program meant ignoring the NCAA was no longer an option. The rules were changing. The NCAA had successfully gotten the upper hand and SMU knew it. Continuing the payment system was not an option.

Option four was to shut down the payment system slowly as the current paid players graduated and no new players were added. This option meant exposing the school to the Death Penalty sanction due to payments occurring after the September 1 date. The players who were paid would theoretically have no reason to turn on SMU and it was possible we could graduate them and wind down the payment system prior to its exposure. It would be risky to choose this option because it could take up to three years to complete. Throughout the entire time, SMU would operate under the threat that any exposed violation would trigger the penalty. It was the only option that offered even a chance of escaping devastating NCAA sanctions.

The leadership knew the options. They debated what penalties we could expect under each scenario. They were all terrible. If we shut down the scheme most likely the NCAA would sanction us in ways that wouldn't be called the *Death Penalty* but would in fact kill us. As a result, the Death Penalty was no longer a deterrent.

The ethics of whether or not to pay was not the issue; it was too late for that. The issue was how much damage the school would incur and who would take responsibility.

It was President Donald Shields' clear responsibility and he did argue to shut it down, but he never gave the order. Athletic Director Bob Hitch was just an employee and very clearly said he would do what he was told. Coach Bobby Collins was also just an employee and he wanted no part in the decision. The only person left was Governor Bill Clements.

So Clements, Chairman of the Board of Governors, former and soon-to-be Governor of Texas weighed the risks versus the costs and made a very rational decision. He made a businessman's decision. He decided it was worth the risk to continue to compensate the existing paid players until they graduated. It was the only chance to avoid a new and even more devastating sanction. Clements decided that there would be no new players added to the payroll and they would hope to get to the 1987 season at which point SMU would finally be clean. He instructed Bob Hitch to make it happen and Bob did.

The NCAA's head of enforcement David Berst, was no dummy. He knew the box SMU was in. After all, he was the guy who constructed it. He figured he could get SMU for either continuing the payment system or for trying to shut it down. It wouldn't matter which. After a few months without a hint of turmoil on SMU's campus, he must have surmised that we chose to keep paying. He was getting closer. He just had to be patient.

Chapter Thirty:
David Stanley

David Stanley was a linebacker from tiny Angleton, Texas. His senior year in high school, he was one of the most devastating players in the country. Off the field he was a loner and socially awkward. On the field he was relentless with hundreds of tackles. His coach designed their defense around him with six linemen up front and Stanley as the single linebacker behind. In 1983 when it came time to recruit him, every college wanted him. It came down to two: SMU and Texas. When SMU outbid Texas, David became a Mustang.

During his first two years he played a bit, but he never had the success that he did in high school. College football at our level was a significant step up and David didn't make it. Around campus he never fit in. SMU could be tough. There were nice cars, plentiful money, connected boys, and beautiful girls. It was an environment David wasn't built for.

For the record, I knew David Stanley as well or better than anybody else at SMU. We had classes together. We practiced and worked out together. David was a bit crazy and very anti-social. He was a year older than me and was already failing on the football field when I met him.

I have no idea why we became quasi-friends, but I can tell you he wasn't friendly and he certainly wasn't looking to be anybody's friend. He was crashing in every way. I would see him at SMU bars in the corner, by himself, drunk. Almost every night he would pick a fight with some fraternity kid. Sometimes they were my fraternity brothers; sometimes they were just unlucky people within reach. Many times I broke up his fights and had to be very careful as he tried to take a swing at me. He was a scary and unpredictable dude.

It was this scary, socially awkward, and formerly great high school athlete that turned to drugs to make it. The more drugs he did, the more unpredictable he became. His football and academics suffered to such a degree that something had to happen. In the spring of 1985, that something was a new NCAA drug testing policy. SMU decided to institute the policy a year earlier than it was required and David got caught up in it. Against NCAA rules, SMU paid for a drug treatment program for him. It didn't work. When he came back from rehab, he was even more bitter. He was convinced the coaches had it in for him. That fall, he played a bit and then his appendix burst ending his season. In the spring of 1986 he withdrew from SMU to try to play for another college.

He asked Dr. Kliever to help him get his affairs in order and then tried to find a school that would have him. It was too late. His high school reputation had been eclipsed by his college results and nobody wanted him. The former Parade All-American that every school in Texas wanted in 1983 was reduced to begging to get back into SMU in 1986. In early summer, he had his mom call Kliever to find out if our 1985 probation prevented him from coming back and if Coach Collins would have him.

After Stanley's mom called Kliever to see if he could re-enroll, Kliever called David Berst to find out the NCAA's policy. Berst knew Stanley was an important recruit from the 1983 SMU recruiting class and was at the heart of many of the alleged violations in recruiting that year. He knew Stanley was bid on by numerous schools and that SMU had won that bidding war. The NCAA interviewed Stanley as part of their

1983-1985 SMU fishing expedition but he never talked of being paid.

Since Stanley was a scholarship player before the 1985 probation, he didn't count as a new scholarship athlete. Berst told Kliever the NCAA had no problem with his re-enrollment as long as he was academically qualified. It was at SMU's discretion whether or not we allowed him back. David Berst didn't get to decide what SMU would do, but he sure could hope.

Chapter Thirty-One:
Stanley Delivered

When David Berst got the call from Lonnie Kliever about David Stanley, his heart must have skipped a beat. The possibility that SMU might deny his readmission was intriguing and definitely worth watching. If Stanley became another disgruntled former SMU player perhaps Berst could use him. But how would he know?

SMU was already on probation for violations during the 1983 and 1984 recruiting classes. The violations were minor with the exception of Sean Stopperich. Without him, there would have been no "smoking gun" and whatever sanctions they would have imposed would have been much less severe.

Berst didn't uncover the payment system but he did successfully hand SMU the harshest penalties in NCAA history. He won and should have moved on to one of the other thirty-plus pending cases on his desk.

As Director of Enforcement, he was responsible for every case the NCAA took on. He understood that allegations against most schools came from biased outside sources. So the allegations alone didn't matter much.

Berst didn't choose which schools had allegations sent in; he had a much bigger role. He got to select from the pile on his desk which of the accused schools the NCAA would pursue. Sometimes, he even got to choose schools without specific allegations against them. Berst decided again that the NCAA wasn't done with SMU.

His problem was that while Stanley had withdrawn from SMU in January 1986, he was trying to re-enroll for the fall. Technically, Stanley was still a student-athlete at SMU. Therefore the NCAA was not allowed to contact him without going through the school. Berst most definitely did not want to alert SMU that he was investigating us. He did not want to interview Stanley on campus with school officials in the room, and he did not want to send a Preliminary Letter of Inquiry. He had to find another way.

The dilemma must have been difficult for Berst. He was a fundamentalist about the NCAA's rules. Zero tolerance. His job was to investigate the NCAA members without causing too much dissention amongst those he policed. It was a delicate job and he had rules too. Within the 435 page NCAA manual outlining all the rules that members had to follow were the rules the NCAA enforcement staff had to follow as well. The rules were clear. The NCAA could not talk to media, they could not talk to a student-athlete without notifying the school, and they could not open an investigation without sending the school a Preliminary Letter of Inquiry first. Berst was planning on breaking those rules, but he felt safe since the NCAA didn't seem to get investigated for their infractions.

Over the years, Berst learned how to investigate a school by selectively leaking information to different media sources. He learned to manipulate and threaten players to get the information he wanted. He learned which schools could be pursued and which schools needed to be handled with kid's gloves. Berst had become very good at his job.

David Berst was hired in 1972 as an enforcement investigator. At the time, the job paid terribly, involved a difficult travel schedule, required interviewing hostile witnesses, and was run by the tyrannical Walter Byers. The only reason to take a job with the NCAA was to get enough experience to be able to quit and sell yourself as someone who could help an accused school navigate the complex NCAA rule book. Investigators rolled in and then rolled out to member schools and conferences rapidly. The only guys who stayed were the true believers. The protégés of Walter Byers. It was a two way street though, Walter Byers had to believe that you viewed NCAA enforcement with the same absolutist zeal he did, or you were out.

Berst stayed and thrived in that environment. Just like Byers, he held grudges and took things personally. The clearest example was his decade's long feud with UNLV's Jerry Tarkanian. Berst ultimately got sanctions against him, but Tarkanian won a $2.5 million out of court settlement against the NCAA for harassment, primarily against Berst.

Berst loved to use the media. In a 1986 Sports Illustrated interview, he was quoted saying, "his people can't do all the work themselves." He continued, "the NCAA increasingly leaves preliminary sleuthing to the press, whose revelations about abuses were then 'catalysts' for NCAA investigations."

In the previous 1983-85 NCAA investigation of SMU, Berst leaked constantly. It had to be him. It could have been Executive Director Walter Byers or Investigator Dan Beebe but Byers didn't talk to media and Beebe hadn't even started on the SMU case when the leaks began. Berst was the only NCAA official that had worked in Dallas prior to 1983 and had the media relationships to pull it off. Later, I think Beebe leaked too but only with the blessing of Byers and Berst.

Thursday March 10, 1983 SMU received an NCAA Preliminary Letter of Inquiry from David Berst opening a new investigation. The letter was sent certified to President L. Donald Shields and nobody outside of Berst's staff in enforcement knew that the letter was sent or its contents. The same day Shields received the letter he received a phone call from John Sparks of WFAA asking about the letter and its contents. Shields was surprised and angry. It was supposed to be confidential. He had not digested the letter and yet here was Sparks with complete knowledge of it. Shields begged off from answering Spark's questions and got the letter.

Sparks' report for WFAA stated who the investigation was centered on and that the recruit had been contacted by the NCAA. That information could only come from the NCAA itself and was not in the confidential letter.

Even though Sparks screwed up by calling President Shields too early, Berst got what he wanted. Forced to comment publicly, Shields put the investigation into the media space for the NCAA and then the NCAA received the additional investigative help of the Dallas sports media. Danny Robbins of the Dallas Times-Herald was the most aggressive but the Dallas Morning News and WFAA joined in.

The NCAA followed up on their confidential leads. They then leaked those leads to the Dallas Times-Herald and others who did their own interviews. The NCAA then sat back with their morning coffee and read about their *confidential* sources in the newspaper. It ended up a joint investigation with the media reporting every move the NCAA made. It was seamless.

Berst leaked the letter to Sparks in hopes that the added pressure of a public investigation would help him get SMU. The goal was to force SMU to respond to media discoveries and investigate itself. SMU chose to ignore the thinly sourced allegations and the NCAA was forced to continue searching for violations they could actually prove.

Over and over again I kept finding stories of confidential NCAA sources and reports leaked to selected media sources and linked to David Berst. When questioned about the leaks, Berst himself seemed unconcerned despite the fact it was his responsibility to protect that information.

Saturday May 26, 1985 The Dallas Morning News reported SMU's football program had been charged with "major

166

violations" by the NCAA and could be hit with tough sanctions, the News quoted an unidentified source as saying the sanctions were mailed from the NCAA to SMU the day before. The leaker went on, "I don't think it's any secret that they're (SMU) involved in major violations."

Thursday August 8, 1985 WFAA reported SMU would not have any scholarships in 1986 and only 15 in 1987. The WFAA story was eight days before the confidential NCAA Infractions Report was released.

Sunday December 18, 1988 KOCO TV announced the contents of a confidential NCAA report on Oklahoma University. The report was not scheduled for release until Monday. Berst said, "FedEx could have mailed a copy of the report sooner than scheduled."

November 1991 U.A.B. AD Gene Bartow wrote a personal and confidential letter to David Berst complaining about NCAA selective enforcement and asking them to investigate the Alabama Basketball program. He was critical of Coach "Bear" Bryant and how the NCAA would not touch him. He noted that several football coaches whose programs had drawn NCAA sanctions--including Jackie Sherrill, Danny Ford and Charley Pell--were "trained" by Bryant.

Bartow's letter was leaked to the Los Angeles Times in 1993 forcing him to back down and apologize. Berst obviously leaked the letter. But an NCAA story about Alabama leaked to a Los Angeles newspaper? I thought that was weird. I checked the byline, Danny Robbins. He was the guy who worked at the Dallas Times-Herald and kept scooping everyone in the 1983 SMU investigation. Then it made sense.

Clearly Berst believed that "his people couldn't do all the work themselves" and he had selected media partners he trusted and used as best he could.

This Stanley thing was tough. Berst wanted him. He knew Stanley had been paid. But there were those rules he was supposed to follow. Then again, Berst just knew SMU was guilty.

He couldn't contact Stanley directly. He needed an indirect way to apply pressure on Stanley to help him become the source he wanted. Leaks had helped in the past; maybe they could again. Berst chose between John Sparks of WFAA and Danny Robbins of the Dallas Times-Herald. TV vs. print. Which would have the biggest impact? Berst went with television and hoped Sparks could do a better job this time.

June 1986, the same month SMU's Kliever alerted Berst that Stanley had withdrawn from SMU and now wanted back in; Berst alerted John Sparks that Stanley might be a disgruntled SMU athlete that he should pursue. It was a safe choice. Sparks believed in protecting sources and would never divulge Berst as the leaker. The only question was, could Sparks turn Stanley against SMU as Berst hoped?

Chapter Thirty-Two:
Sparks v. Stanley

Sparks was no rookie. He knew a leak of this caliber was a big deal. He knew the NCAA was a biased source and that they leaked Stanley's information for their own purposes. He also knew it was against NCAA rules for Berst to leak such information. If Stanley could be turned against SMU his allegations would lead directly to SMU being handed the Death Penalty. Not disclosing a biased source was a breach of his journalistic ethics, but an exclusive on an NCAA Death Penalty case was a once-in-a-lifetime story. So Sparks took the leak from his biased source and began his chase.

He called Stanley's parents in hopes of talking to him. At first Stanley avoided him, and then he gradually warmed up. Sparks asked him about SMU and his hopes of playing. He asked about SMU allowing him back on the team. And he asked about being paid. Stanley still had hopes that SMU would take him back. He lied to Sparks. Repeatedly. He didn't tell him anything about being paid. Sparks kept at him over the summer months hoping that Stanley would turn. Stanley continued to tell him nothing.

As August approached, Stanley was out of time. If Coach Collins was going to let him play, he had to have the answer now. Kliever told Stanley that Collins didn't want him back because "he abandoned the team after the recent probation and that it would send a bad message to the rest of the team." The real reason was Stanley was a drug addicted player that didn't have the ability to play at our level. His negative behavior was also a bad influence on our team. Collins was glad to have him gone. We all were.

Stanley needed to know for sure. I remember the day he came to practice to catch Coach Collins. It was surreal. Rumors flew around practice that Stanley just showed up. I saw him across the field, I saw him talking to Collins, and I saw him walk away. He came over to a few of us and we talked about what he was doing. He wanted to be allowed back on the team and was told "no." He wasn't mad and seemed serious. We asked him what he was going to do. He said he "didn't know." Then he walked off the field. I didn't think about him again until the rumors started the week of the Texas game. But it was that day and that moment that David Stanley became a threat to our program, no earlier.

In a Sports Illustrated article dated March 9, 1987 Sparks said he received an anonymous tip from within the athletic department about alleged payments. However, in an interview about the Death Penalty in The SMU Daily Campus dated November 9, 2009 he stated that "he received a tip from a former staff member of The Daily Campus about a player receiving money under the table at SMU." So the producer for WFAA who broke the David Stanley story had two conflicting anonymous sources for his tip.

The athletic staffer was obviously Theresa Hawthorne. She was fired June 1985 for cause and was angry. She knew some things about our program and contacted media sources to hurt us. We paid out her $17,500 contract in early 1986 and she signed statements that she knew of no NCAA violations. Theresa didn't have any information about David Stanley that was meaningful in the critical time period of June-October 1986. She was long gone. She might have known Stanley "was a paid player" in 1985. So what? Stanley didn't turn and become a legitimate source until October 1986.

The fact that WFAA threw her out there back then as their source showed that they knew they had a problem. They needed a credible way to say they discovered Stanley. The fact that she had no way to be their source got lost in the story as it quickly grew and left their lie behind. That WFAA used the Theresa lie in 1986 was understandable. That Dale Hansen referenced her again in the "Pony Excess" film as his source was shameless. That John Sparks would not participate in the film or reference her as his source was interesting.

I contacted Sparks about Stanley. I asked him how he found Stanley. I already knew Stanley didn't contact him first. Based on other interviews Sparks gave back then, I knew he started pursuing Stanley months before he turned on SMU. I also knew how few people could have known Stanley was a potentially disgruntled player over the summer. Sparks had a problem. His timeline didn't work. He and Hansen tried to sell Theresa as the person who tipped them but that was laughable. I mentioned the conflicting accounts. Which was it? He said that it was true; a newspaper staffer "confirmed" to him that players were still being paid after the 1985 infractions report. I didn't ask that.

What about Stanley? Sparks wanted to know why I was interested. I told him I knew Stanley and had trouble with how Sparks found him. Would he clarify? His response indicated that he looked me up. He asked if I transferred after the Death Penalty. I told him "no" and again asked how he found Stanley. His answer was perfect. He said his role as a journalist was protected by the First Amendment to the U.S. Constitution and the role of the press was central to our freedom and way of life. He said he valued the role of his confidential source and would not disclose him. He also said he would "leave it up to me and my guesses as to who it was." I laughed and told him I thought that was a great answer. I already knew it was Berst but he just confirmed it for me and didn't even know it.

It's been twenty-five years since WFAA broke the story. They have continuously defended themselves that they were just good reporters following leads and pursuing a good story. They milked the story for awards, prestige, and increased ratings. Through it all they have stated how important it was to get the truth out, that the integrity of the story was paramount, that they were proud of their hard work. And yet, they cannot answer one simple question. How and why did they start to chase David Stanley in June 1986 four months before he turned on SMU and talked?

Chapter Thirty-Three:
Berst v. NCAA Bylaws

As the 1986 season opened, the NCAA had no knowledge of whether or not Stanley was on the team. SMU had three road games in a row and did not travel the entire team. Like every other college team, our roster was on file at our athletic office. But no way was anyone at the NCAA going to request a copy of it and alert SMU that they were looking around again. So Berst waited. He waited until October 4 which was our first home game against Boston College. At that game our entire team suited up and David Stanley wasn't on the sidelines.

Now Berst knew that Stanley wasn't on our team and that he was the potentially disgruntled former SMU player he had been hoping for. But still Berst waited. SMU had done nothing wrong. There was no reason to pursue us. According to Berst, the NCAA "wasn't a police department" and "wasn't out looking for violators." They only "initiated an investigation because information comes to us."

But we won three of our first four games and that wasn't supposed to happen. The whole point of the NCAA enforcement mechanism was to show that the NCAA was in charge and could knock a program down sufficiently to prove cheating wasn't worth it. SMU wasn't playing along. The following week after we upset #13 Baylor and were ranked #20, Berst must have been hopping mad. Not only were we winning despite the worst sanctions ever handed down, we were ranked again. On October 18 we beat Houston and moved up in the rankings to #18.

It was that win that spurred Berst into action. We were 5-1 and scheduled to play a very average Texas team the following Saturday and were expected to win again. Another win against a high profile team would have moved us up to #15 or higher and would have embarrassed the NCAA even more. Berst decided to take matters into his own hands.

He knew Sparks was chasing Stanley, but so far Stanley had not talked. If he never admitted being paid, WFAA could not run a story, and the NCAA would have no allegations to respond to.

Even though he could finally interview Stanley without having to notify SMU, it was a questionable call. The Rules of Procedure stated that he was supposed to send SMU a Preliminary Letter of Inquiry *before* he opened an investigation or dispatched a field investigator to interview witnesses. Berst's loophole was that he was allowed to evaluate information to determine if there might be sufficient evidence that would warrant an investigation.

The evaluation phase usually occurred in Berst's office as he determined who to investigate. The investigation phase occurred in the field as he tried to gather evidence to prove an allegation. With SMU he was long past the general information phase and was now seeking specific evidence.

There were no media reports of any wrongdoing. David Stanley had done nothing to attract attention and had not contacted the NCAA. There was no official reason to send an investigator to SMU. Numerous other schools had actual allegations pending against them according to Berst himself and yet somehow, Berst decided that SMU should be moved back to the top of the list ahead of them all. Why? Because we were winning and David was mad.

He made the decision to send Butch Worley to Dallas to interview David Stanley without following the rules. Berst was obviously deep into an unauthorized secret investigation of SMU, but as long as he could argue he was just trying to determine if an infraction had occurred, he could send the required letter later. Who would ever know?

Chapter Thirty-Four:
Sherwood says "No"

Sherwood Blount Jr., better known as Ol' Sherwood as he refers to himself, was a complex man. The son of a fireman from middle class East Dallas, in 1968 he turned down the opportunity to play professional baseball in favor of a football scholarship to SMU. He joined the Alpha Tau Omega (ATO) fraternity and was popular on campus. By 1969 he earned the starting middle linebacker position and was eventually awarded team co-captain honors. During his senior year he was invited to play in the East-West Shrine Game where all the best college players were allowed a final all-star game. Numerous NFL scouts were in attendance. It was a big honor for Sherwood and was viewed as a potential launching pad to a career in the NFL. But he chose a different path.

His coach, Hayden Fry, offered him a coaching job upon graduation but Sherwood was more interested in making money. Dallas in the early 1970's was rocking, especially real estate. Everywhere you looked there was construction. Dallas was building single family homes and apartments for the multitudes moving in, expanding and leasing office buildings for where they would work, and developing shopping malls for where they would spend their money. Sherwood worked hard and amassed a fortune in real estate just a few short years after graduation. All accounts of him noted his strong work ethic and also his larger than life ego.

Sherwood greatly enjoyed being around SMU football and he liked Ron Meyer. They both believed SMU football could be great again and were willing to work hard to make it happen. From this mutual interest, Sherwood began to help recruit players. There were other boosters that helped and there were other boosters from other schools they competed against. But Sherwood attacked recruiting with a vengeance just as he pursued football and real estate transactions. He enjoyed the challenge.

By the time Ron Meyer left in 1982 and Bobby Collins replaced him, the boosters felt themselves extensions of the coaching staff.

The 1983 recruiting wars were a reflection of several factors: the aggressive Ron Meyer leaving SMU, his replacement with the laid back Bobby Collins, and then the graduation of their spectacular 1979 class. All this combined with a fear it would unwind should they be unable to reproduce that monster class. The entire conference seemed to get the memo. It was war! All the schools, every booster and all the players jumped in. By the time it was over, SMU had signed the #6 class in the country and pissed off the entire conference in doing so.

In the resulting investigation, it was Sherwood Blount who was named as the primary booster responsible for paying Sean Stopperich (recruit #1), the only major violation the NCAA could prove.

After the NCAA report, President Shields and other SMU officials repeatedly said the violations were the fault of uncontrolled boosters. It wasn't true, but it was the story that was pushed and they stuck to it. From Sherwood's perspective he had done what SMU had asked of him and was then tossed overboard when things became too hot. The strange part is that he seemed to understand it was only an act and didn't take it personally. He remained a loyal SMU supporter and booster even though he was supposedly banned.

When Bob Hitch approached him to continue funding the payment scheme until it could be wound down, he agreed. He would end up contributing over $61,000 to this fund though he was not allowed to talk to players, coaches, or athletic staff. He was not allowed in the locker room, the team plane, or on the sidelines. In fact, all the old perks of being a big time booster were gone, yet he still contributed when he was asked to.

In August 1986, Sherwood was contacted by David Stanley. Sherwood had recently been the sole funding source for the payments and Stanley was looking to get paid. When Coach Collins told Stanley he was not welcome back on the team, it was devastating to Stanley. Now he knew. He could not get a scholarship with another school and SMU would not have him. He was done and went looking for a severance package. He had valuable information against SMU and he was determined to sell it.

I read about Stanley trying to extort $150,000 from Sherwood and I asked him recently if it was true. He repeatedly said "no comment." We talked for forty-five minutes and he told me many things but he would not speak about that. We exchanged emails and he shared some opinions but for the most part he wouldn't confirm or deny my conclusions.

What I know is that in August and again in September, Sherwood Blount wrote to Bill Clements, Chairman of SMU's Board of Governors, to complain about SMU's blaming the boosters for all the athletic department's problems. Sherwood wanted a meeting. Clements finally agreed to meet with Sherwood, Sherwood's attorney and SMU's attorney on October 20, 1986 at Clements' office. The meeting has been presented as an opportunity for Sherwood to air his grievances about his treatment in the media by President Shields. But I think the real reason was Sherwood was afraid.

178

Afraid because previously in 1985, he was singled out and then blamed for all the NCAA violations. Now in 1986 when Stanley approached him for money, Sherwood recognized the trap. If he paid Stanley, it would never end. That was not an option. If he turned Stanley down and Stanley went public, SMU would be investigated again, and Sherwood would be blamed again. He had agreed to fund the payment system through a private arrangement with Bob Hitch. Nobody else knew he had been asked to provide the funds. If the story came out, he would be the fall guy, and Sherwood knew it.

At their meeting Sherwood did ask that President Shields tone down the negative comments regarding himself and the other boosters. But he also got on record that Bill Clements not only knew about, but authorized and requested the payments he had been making. Armed with that little bit of insurance, Sherwood Blount told David Stanley "No" to the extortion demand.

While Blount delayed answering Stanley in late August and throughout September until he could get his meeting with Clements, Stanley was delaying a meeting of his own. The day after getting Sherwood's answer, Stanley agreed to meet with NCAA Assistant Director of Enforcement Butch Worley and started talking.

Chapter Thirty-Five:
Berst goes Rogue

Stanley was pissed. He wanted money and he couldn't figure out how to get it. When Sherwood told him "no" to the extortion demand after leading him on for over a month, he was running out of options. He could go to the media perhaps. But how much would they pay? He decided to raise the pressure on SMU and see what would happen. Butch Worley of the NCAA had been trying to set up a meeting so he agreed to see him.

He told Worley he was paid $25,000 to attend SMU back in 1983 and received monthly payments while he was enrolled through December 1985. He talked of other players with similar payment arrangements, but he gave no player names. Worley tried to sweeten the pot by offering him immunity to testify against SMU, but no schools had shown interest in him so it didn't really matter. Stanley told Worley that he would not testify against SMU nor sign a statement.

According to NCAA rules, an athlete's allegations are just that until he provides evidence to back them up and then attests and gives the NCAA the right to use his evidence. If the evidence is not proven within the rules of the NCAA by-laws, the evidence and thus the violation never happened. The only thing Stanley gave the NCAA was an un-provable allegation from a drop out and a drug addict. It was enough to open a formal investigation and nothing more. Stanley thought maybe that kind of pressure would get SMU's attention.

The NCAA set Stanley's oral allegations on the table and took a deep breath. For the NCAA to convict SMU, Stanley's statement wasn't sufficient and it was questionable that it would even be up for discussion with the Infractions Committee. They needed more. Another problem was the fact that SMU was eligible for the newly enacted repeat violator statute, the Death Penalty. As such, this case would be highly scrutinized. There could be no NCAA screw up or questionable violation if they were to secure the penalty. And make no mistake, they wanted that penalty.

David Berst must have spent numerous hours with Executive Director Walter Byers, debating their next steps. These two guys, who were charged with enforcing a strict set of rules on their membership, were now discussing how to break more rules to catch us. The irony was that they were both described as absolutists when dealing with member violations. Yet, they were more flexible and didn't seem to care that they were violating their own rules in the pursuit of SMU.

And this was when the NCAA found themselves in a trap of their own. They knew SMU had been cheating past the September 1, 1985 Death Penalty date but they had no evidence. They were consumed knowing our slush fund continued over the last decade despite two separate investigations. They needed for the NCAA to demonstrate its power in the wake of the CFA and the existential threat it presented. They wanted to drop a bomb to prove they could clean up all the rampant cheating. So they conspired to create a scenario and an enemy to drop that bomb on.

The whole point of the penalty was to use it and scare everybody else straight. If Stanley wouldn't attest to his statement or allow its use, how could they obtain the evidence they needed to impose the Death Penalty? They spent years in the last investigation. If they followed the rules and opened another investigation, they could expect even more resistance from SMU this time. Due to the nature of the more serious penalty we faced, SMU would surely fight to the death.

Berst was faced with three options. He could end the secret investigation and wait for usable evidence. If he did that, we might have wound down the payment scheme before he got another chance at us. He rejected that option. He had enough evidence to send a Letter of Inquiry and open a formal investigation. It would have been a repeat of the previous twenty-nine month investigation and he had no witness or evidence to start, but he would be following NCAA rules. Or, he could try a new version of an old tactic.

He could try to manufacture a media event that would force SMU to have to investigate itself. The advantage was he would not have to conduct interviews, build a case, or follow NCAA rules. His fingerprints wouldn't be on anything. The disadvantage was that he couldn't be sure the event would be sufficient to force us to self-investigate and disclose any violations. Another disadvantage of course, was that it was against NCAA rules to setup a member school.

Berst chose to break more NCAA bylaws and helped create a media event in order to force SMU to have to investigate itself. He cheated to catch a cheater. It made total sense.

But as I read and re-read the NCAA manual, I couldn't find any rule that said it was okay for the NCAA to break its own rules in pursuit of a rule breaker. It didn't say that some violations were so serious that the bylaws could be ignored. It didn't say that a repeat violator could be pursued in any fashion because they were a serious threat to college athletics. No, the manual very clearly laid out the procedures for catching and penalizing a rule breaker, all rule breakers; procedures Berst chose not to follow.

Based on how the NCAA leaked to the media in the previous investigation, they needed to raise the stakes. The numerous leaks planted in the usual outlets did not spur SMU into self-disclosing that time. This time, he decided a TV event would be better to create outrage and a resulting SMU response.

He had already leaked the information about Stanley to John Sparks at WFAA and John had worked on Stanley all summer with no result. Now things were different. While Stanley didn't tell the NCAA anything they could use, he did tell them enough for the media to use.

If Stanley would just repeat his claims to WFAA, Berst might yet get the media event he craved. He was breaking numerous NCAA rules now but it was the only way to catch us. He had to do it. The NCAA rules be damned, he was going to get his whale.

Chapter Thirty-Six:
Stanley gets Angry

Stanley was not sure what he was doing. He initially wanted to play for another team that would give him a second chance. When that didn't materialize, he came back to SMU for a third chance. When Coach Collins shut down that option, he went for the money from Sherwood Blount. When Sherwood shut him down, he started to sell his story to the media. While he was trying to sell his story, the NCAA showed up. It was good timing for the NCAA and bad timing for Stanley. He hadn't sold his story yet and now the NCAA was pressing.

After meeting with Butch Worley, Stanley had to act fast. If the NCAA were to break the story or leak it, his information would become worthless. He needed to sell it to SMU or to the media. Giving it to the NCAA or to the media for free was a non-starter. WFAA was first in line due to Sparks working on him all summer. Somehow they were able to give him enough. Stanley revised the story he had been telling them to now include details of SMU's payment system and the payments he received.

The information alone wasn't enough for much of a story. A former drug addicted player alleges that he was paid to attend SMU and received payments after enrolling. It would be a he said/she said story, make for some bad publicity, and then be over. But Stanley gave Sparks a couple of postmarked empty SMU envelopes that he said contained the cash he received. Even that evidence didn't mean much. The envelopes could have contained any normal correspondence that SMU sent players. But if WFAA could surprise SMU officials while on camera, perhaps they could create a media event.

Sparks called AD Bob Hitch and set up a taped interview about recruiting for Monday, October 27 just six days after Stanley talked to Butch Worley and two days after our last second loss to Texas in Austin. He didn't want to talk about the Texas game and he didn't want to talk about our new offensive style or how well we were playing. No, he wanted to talk about recruiting.

I have always wondered about that interview. I wondered why SMU agreed to the interview and I wondered how we could fumble it so badly. After piecing my memories and the timeline together, I'm now convinced SMU knew WFAA would ask about Stanley and they thought they were prepared with an answer.

Hitch and Coach Collins knew denying Stanley a roster spot in August was risky and knew he would potentially turn on us. If all of us players knew Stanley was out there pissed off, so did they. SMU also knew it was highly irregular to send a film crew along with John Sparks and Dale Hansen to tape an interview about recruiting. It was in the middle of the season after a tough loss to Texas. And it was at a time of year when a coach would never disclose the recruits he was interested in. What possible recruiting information was so newsworthy?

While recruiting was the reason Sparks gave to Hitch when he requested the interview, his personnel requests were even more extraordinary. He asked for the Athletic Director (who had nothing to do with recruiting), the Head Coach (who was in the middle of the football season and not allowed to recruit), and the assistant AD in charge of recruiting logistics (who approved the expense reports for the coaches who did recruit), to all be in the interview. Those three guys? In one room? In the middle of the season? To talk about recruiting? Not possible.

But the fact is, they agreed to the interview even though they knew Sparks didn't just do sports stories. He was WFAA's Investigative Journalist. They must have suspected Stanley had talked and they must have thought the story was going to get out anyway. So they sat down ready to call Stanley a disgruntled former player who was a drug addict and a liar. With two other SMU officials next them, each one must have felt comfortable that they had it under control. They didn't.

Sparks and Hansen knew on October 27 right after the interview was over that they had a gold mine. Anyone watching the tape with an unbiased eye would have to admit it looked bad for SMU. In fact it was devastating. But I think the worst thing that came out of the interview was that SMU's plan to trash Stanley made things worse. Remember, Stanley told the NCAA he was paid yet said they couldn't use his information. He then told Sparks the same story and gave him the envelopes that Hansen used to embarrass Parker. It was nowhere near enough and Sparks had work to do.

WFAA delayed airing the October 27 interview until mid-November to give them time to nail down the story. Only the WFAA crew and SMU staff knew that Hitch called Stanley a drug addict and a liar during the taped interview.

After the interview, Sparks told Stanley that SMU would now have to destroy his credibility. He used Hitch's comments to manipulate Stanley into a rage against Hitch. Stanley became determined to prove that what he said was true and that what Hitch said was the lie. Sparks played it up. It was all true that Stanley was a disgruntled former player who was a drug addict. But he wasn't a liar...this time. He had that going for him.

Sparks made sure to keep the NCAA informed of how it went. According to the Houston Chronicle, David Berst "was told of Stanley's charges on October 27, the day WFAA confronted SMU officials" and sixteen days before the story aired.

Stanley then took lie detector tests and told Sparks everything in detail and on camera. We made him mad and Sparks encouraged him to get even. WFAA was on ethical thin ice. Journalists were not supposed to become part of their stories, but at this point WFAA and Sparks were creating the story as much as covering it.

Then came November 1986. The story aired. After Stanley's allegations and the devastating interview of Hitch, Collins and Parker exploded across television sets, the SMU community exploded too. Students and faculty were outraged and SMU's leaders were confused. Nobody seemed to know how to respond to the daily accusations of wrongdoing. The scandal began to spin out of control. We players were confused too and just tried to hang on. For the NCAA, things couldn't have been more perfect.

Chapter Thirty-Seven:
No Way Out – Strike Two

The WFAA story had the NCAA's intended effect on the SMU administration and athletic staff. It scared the hell out of them. The leak to Sparks at WFAA offered an end-around for Berst. WFAA rattled SMU's cage and the NCAA planned to simply ask SMU to clarify all those "disturbing" reports. Berst would not open an investigation. He would not be bound by the rules of the Infractions Committee. He would simply push from outside the rules and see what happened.

When SMU's Kliever called Berst after the WFAA interview but before it was broadcast to inform him that SMU might have a violation to investigate, Berst gave just the right shove back. He said, "I'm glad you called to inform us. But you should know we already know all about Stanley and we know a whole lot more too." The well-intentioned Kliever was no match for the game being played. He thought the NCAA's Berst was his buddy. He figured if SMU just followed the rules, Berst would make sure we were treated fairly. What Kliever never understood was the game was all about creating sufficient fear for us to disclose everything and then the NCAA would "grudgingly" shut us down. They would have no choice you know, since the SMU football program was just too corrupt to save.

Stanley's initial allegations weren't major because he was just one guy who was paid by a booster back in 1983. Stanley now alleged that he was paid after the September 1, 1985 trigger date for the Death Penalty. He also alleged he was paid by an SMU athletic staffer instead of a booster. That was different and brought the payment scheme inside SMU. But Stanley couldn't prove any of it. So the NCAA had an allegation they couldn't use and WFAA had a news report that was all sizzle and no substance.

Despite the unverifiable nature of Stanley's allegations, SMU was in full crisis mode. Our recent probation had exposed none of the payments and none of the roles of athletic department officials. We had blamed it all on boosters and now it was exposed that there were in fact SMU officials involved.

Berst knew he needed more. He told Kliever that the "most troubling thing" was that SMU paid for Stanley's drug treatment the previous spring. And ominously he was "surprised" that even President Donald Shields was involved in approving the payment for the drug treatment.

There was no way the NCAA would have penalized us for helping an athlete with a drug problem. But Shields and SMU were exposed with another non-disclosed violation. Berst played it up. He "hoped there was a good explanation" for SMU authorizing the treatment money and for President Shields signing the NCAA compliance forms stating they had broken no rules. That was the end of Shields. He resigned the following week.

By late November, there was still no open investigation and the NCAA had done nothing more than interview Stanley back in October. They were just pushing buttons and pulling levers behind the scenes. It was brilliant.

On SMU's campus, the collateral damage was still being assessed. After Shields left, Athletic Director Bob Hitch resigned, then Head Coach Bobby Collins and Associate Athletic Director Henry Lee Parker followed suit. One day I woke up and all of our coaches and athletic staff were gone. In place, we only had our strength and conditioning coach for guidance. It was not a very comforting scene.

SMU gave Dr. Kliever the additional responsibility to act as our team leader. Everybody else was gone. He was in charge. So the fifty-seven players that still had eligibility after the 1986 season sat and listened as he explained how we were going to deal with the crisis. He told us that SMU knew full well that further NCAA infractions could trigger the so-called "Death Penalty." That the school was done screwing around and we would internally investigate the allegations, self-disclose all infractions, and throw ourselves on the mercy of the NCAA. Kliever even went so far as to call a team meeting on behalf of the NCAA and asked us players to testify against SMU in exchange for immunity. That made no sense to us. But it did make sense to the NCAA. At that time, they had no usable evidence. Perhaps we players could still be manipulated.

We sat there stunned as Dr. Kliever told us we were going to tell the NCAA everything in hopes of leniency. We were upset and thought Kliever was nuts. We knew the NCAA was not our friend. We were young and had no power to decide what SMU was going to do, but we fully understood that the results were going to disproportionately affect us. If the NCAA gave us death, it was us who would be killed. The administration and faculty would continue on as before.

If we told everything, the Death Penalty was a certainty. If we lied, we took the chance that the NCAA would find out anyway, but there was a chance of survival. To us it was suicide to tell everything. There would be no mercy in this environment. The NCAA was looking for scalps not a truce. SMU marched forward.

We did not want the NCAA to conduct their own investigation, and neither did they. We wanted to control the information released, and they didn't want to have to start following the *Rules of Procedure*. So Dr. Kliever offered to lead an internal investigation, and the NCAA happily sat back and watched as we devoured our self. The deal was simple: we would investigate, disclose what we found, and admit to our guilt. If the NCAA was unhappy with our results, they could throw out our confession and open their own investigation.

In early February 1987, we delivered our internal findings to the NCAA. We did not disclose the names of the players, athletic staff, members of the SMU community, or boosters that were involved. We did self-disclose thirteen players that received $47,000 during the 1985-86 school year. Eight of those players still had eligibility during the 1986 season and received an additional $14,000 during those five months. It averaged out to between $300 and $400 per month per athlete. Three of those eight players still had eligibility going into the 1987 season.

We also admitted that "senior athletic department" officials were aware of the payments. The David Stanley allegations that WFAA had breathlessly reported were not included in our report. That was the sum total of the investigation we offered to the NCAA and they could take it or leave it.

Those numbers matched my knowledge of how it worked. The rumors about thousands and thousands of dollars were simply lies and exaggerations. Some recruits got "signing bonuses" in prior years but in the matter of enrolled student-athletes, the payments were simply amounts sufficient to help the poorest players cover the incidentals that a scholarship didn't.

Berst didn't like it. He wanted the names of all those involved; he wanted more details. He chased us for over a decade to get to this point and it was unsatisfying. He knew there was more to the story but he did not want to start an official NCAA investigation without SMU's cooperation or witnesses. So he took the deal.

Once the NCAA had the report from SMU agreed to and signed off by SMU as accurate, the NCAA Committee on Infractions could now determine our penalty.

This phase was what all the cooperation was for. The NCAA never had any evidence against us, but they had us scared and without leadership. In this environment, we were manipulated to disclose information that the NCAA would never have found. The payoff for SMU was to be leniency. Now to be fair, the NCAA never promised leniency, but they sure did infer it. We bent over backwards to give them everything. In doing so, we worked out an arrangement to avoid the Death Penalty. Yet, when our report was presented to the Infractions Committee, they decided to throw out the enforcement staff's recommended penalties and the deal for leniency along with them.

On February 25, 1987 the Committee looked at all the evidence, considered all that had gone on at SMU and was currently going on in the world of college football, and decided to send a message. Death. But because we cooperated so well, because we gave them everything, they only killed us for one-year instead of the two-year Death Penalty they were allowed. That was a nice gesture but it was irrelevant. Dead was dead. The length of time of our death was less important than whether or not we were dead. And there was no doubt, they killed us. Everybody associated with the program was fired. All boosters associated with the scandal were banned. All players were released. There was no program and nobody left.

From this modified Death Penalty eliminating the 1987 season, SMU cancelled the 1988 season because we wouldn't have had enough players to field a team. The net result was the same as if the NCAA had assessed us the full two-year penalty. We gained nothing by cooperating with the NCAA, while they gained everything and could finally display their hard-earned trophy.

Chapter Thirty-Eight:
The University of Texas Investigations

I looked into SMU's previous investigations and felt that all the outrage aimed at our program was largely over-blown. For years I had heard that Texas did everything we did and more, but because they were a large and politically connected public school, they were untouchable. Well, I didn't know and I decided to find out. No more rumors, what were the facts?

The University of Texas in Austin is the largest state university in Texas. They have always enjoyed a privileged position in Texas because of their size and the large number of alumni that remain in the state. When Lyndon Baines Johnson was president from 1963 through 1968, he regularly sent his helicopter to bring coaches and players to his ranch to get game information from them. It also didn't hurt in the recruiting battles to have such a high ranking official drop-ping by and meeting recruits.

From 1957 through 1976 Darrell Royal served as head coach. He was also the AD from 1962 through 1980. As the coach at a big time football school for so long, he witnessed the tremendous growth of college football at the same time the NCAA tried to manage it all. He was a longtime friend of the NCAA's Walter Byers.

The most interesting allegation of Texas cheating came in the 1964 Cotton Bowl. The game pitted undefeated #1 Texas against Roger Staubach's #2 Navy (their only loss an upset in the same Cotton Bowl against SMU). Texas won the game 28 – 6 and with it their first National Championship. But after the game it was revealed that Texas had somehow gotten the Navy sideline signals before the game. There was no NCAA investigation.

The first time UT got into trouble with the NCAA was later in 1964. They were found guilty of major recruiting violations by putting visiting recruits in hotels and giving them per diem cash money for meals. The recruits were allowed to charge meals to their hotel and keep the per diem money. UT also paid for the meals for friends who accompanied the recruits on their visits. One recruit was transported to and from his home to Austin in a private airplane. The NCAA made note of Texas' cooperation and placed them on probation for one year with no TV or postseason penalties.

This was a bit more serious than SMU's investigation in 1965 where we gave two student-athletes a ride home and back to school in a private plane. The NCAA also made note of the cooperation we provided yet gave us two years' probation and a one-year ban on postseason play. Didn't seem like equal treatment right off the bat, but I kept looking.

In 1974, Texas' second NCAA investigation never happened. Media reported several UT athletes were receiving pay for working in the Capitol but rarely showed up for work. Texas was allowed to conduct its own investigation and the NCAA never sent an investigator to Austin. Case closed. Hmmm.

In 1980, Royal retired as AD and a year later, Deloss Dodds was hired. Dodds was an even better friend of Byers and had gotten his start in administration through Byers. Previously, he worked at the NCAA and was a member of the Rules Committee.

The third Texas investigation was in 1982 and it was for recruiting violations and the sale of complimentary football tickets by a student athlete. He sold fourteen tickets to a booster at a price *substantially* in excess of face value. The NCAA didn't spend much time on it and determined that the sale of the tickets was an "isolated event and did not involve institutional personnel." Two assistant coaches arranged for cowboy boots to be given to a recruit. It was determined that the recruiting violation was minor and the coaches were scolded. UT was reprimanded and placed on probation for one year. No other penalties or sanctions were imposed on the school. The team was immediately eligible for television appearances and postseason bowl appearances. No way would SMU have gotten off that light.

The fourth NCAA investigation again never happened. In September 1986, forty-six UT players were exposed for having arranged free passes to the first two football games of the 1985 season for non-family members (aka: boosters). Players at the Universities of Nebraska and Tennessee had also been caught giving their passes out and were suspended by the NCAA for one to two games. Deloss Dodds said the Texas free passes were "trivial" and that he was not going to turn in his players for the probable suspensions.

The use of free passes was a new rule implemented for the 1985 season to prevent players from having tickets to sell at inflated prices to boosters. The SWC sponsored the rule change in response to allegations that Texas' players had been selling their tickets for years. Dodds did not report the violation to the NCAA and the NCAA chose not to investigate.

Then in March 1986, The Dallas Morning News led a two-month investigation of the Texas football program and released their findings in the form of a detailed expose. In the report, former players alleged that boosters and agents, whom they usually met through coaches, routinely approached players with cash and favors. They interviewed twenty-eight players whose careers spanned the years of 1978 to 1985. Eleven said they accepted cash payments amounting to as much as $10,000 and that alumni would walk up to players in the locker room and then shake hands leaving hundreds in the player's hand. The DMN also reported that twenty-four of the twenty-eight players routinely sold their complimentary game tickets to boosters at dramatically inflated prices. Most players said they received about $4,000 per season from the ticket sales with some saying they made that much just from selling their annual Texas-Oklahoma tickets. Team wide ticket sales seemed to be the main way the team financed their players' slush fund.

Many of the players said they established long term relationships with their "sugar daddies" and received regular payments. Beyond cash payments, seventeen of the twenty-eight players said they were given "beer and liquor, rides to their hometowns and back to campus, and freebies at Austin restaurants and nightclubs." One booster founded a black professional's association to provide free legal, medical and dental services to black players. They even had a club *Phases,* Austin's only black nightclub, which was owned by the association and provided free cover, food, and drinks to the players.

The allegations went on and on. Limo rides, stacks of cash at strip clubs, dinner parties for players and their families, half-price apartments, and sometimes tens of thousands of dollars to a player who "really stood out." The players and the boosters had no apologies for the payment plans. In the articles, the UT boosters and players were clear that the poor players needed the money to make it and that they would continue to take the money until the NCAA provided some type of allowance.

Even though the players said that they were introduced to their "sugar daddies" by coaches and at UT events, Head Coach Fred Akers said he was surprised that all this cash was floating around but that "...no college coach can completely

196

control alumni and agents." Meanwhile, most of the "cash handshakes" occurred in the locker rooms after the games and in the presence of the coaches.

Wow! It was the mother lode. It was huge and the NCAA could not ignore it. All of Texas' connections could not make this massive scandal go away. There would have to be a full investigation and Texas would have to be treated like any other program that had significant major violations disclosed in the media.

Oddly, it took the NCAA a year to get around to it…and a lot could happen in a year.

Chapter Thirty-Nine:
The NCAA Hammers U.T.

The 1986 season was about to start. Earlier in the year, we had suffered through the loss of our entire recruiting class and then we read about the allegations at Texas. We were sure that Texas would be joining us soon with significant penalties. Yet all was quiet. Months drifted by without any news. There was no response from the NCAA and there were no leaks of any investigation. That was okay. It was supposed to be confidential.

Texas got through the entire 1986 season, they signed a good recruiting class in February 1987 and then in March with the recruiting class firmly tucked away, the NCAA finally sent them a Preliminary Letter of Inquiry. That letter did indicate the NCAA had opened an investigation into the Texas football program, but the letter and their alleged violations got lost in the media frenzy surrounding the release of SMU's Death Penalty report. SMU and death were all anyone was reporting on. No one had the time to cover the Texas probe. That one year delay by the NCAA was helpful.

The NCAA then decided to allow UT to investigate itself and use an attorney who was a former UT football player as the investigator. He was to report his findings to the NCAA. The point man from the NCAA assisting the UT lawyer was Butch Worley. Worley was the guy who had just wrapped up investigating SMU. He was a recent Texas Tech law school graduate who openly proclaimed that his dream job was to work for the athletic department of UT. Getting Worley to investigate them was also helpful for Texas.

The violations presented by the internal UT investigation and signed off by the NCAA included: seventeen instances of coaches giving recruits money on recruiting visits, sixteen instances of coaches loaning players cars, and fifteen instances of coaches "loaning" players cash, coaches lying on compliance forms over a four-year period about breaking NCAA rules. Head Coach David McWilliams admitted paying players for gas, loaning out his personal car, and arranging lower rent for players than market rents. Assistant Coach and recruiting coordinator Ken Dabbs carried large amounts of cash and gave it to numerous players for "miscellaneous purposes." Numerous other assistant coaches either gave cash or arranged for "loans."

The report went on: jerseys and meals bought for recruits, between 1980-85 numerous players sold their complimentary tickets far in excess of face value, a coach arranged a private plane ride home on a booster's plane for a student-athlete and gave him $150 spending money, several coaches gave student-athletes the free use of their cars, a booster employed a recruit right before he signed his letter of intent with Texas until the recruit graduated from high school while an assistant coach knew all the details, a booster arranged and paid for an annual pre-season party for student-athletes where drinks and meals were provided, boosters also provided meals and clothes over a ten-year period for numerous athletes, meals and cash were provided to student-athletes at Austin restaurants, and the head and assistant coaches provided false certification of compliance forms to the NCAA during the 1983, 84, 85, and 86 seasons.

Based on the false statements by the coaches, the University President erroneously certified the university's compliance with NCAA legislation. The report also mentioned eight boosters as having given cash inducements to players but only one, who was also a professional sports agent, was asked to disassociate himself from the UT athletic department.

Texas' excuse to the NCAA was this: there was no organized scheme among coaches or the athletic department to have the players sell their inflated football tickets, there were no "regular" payments to athletes, there were no cars or cash payments to get players to sign with UT, and that there was no "evidence" of a slush fund.

The NCAA recognized the cooperative approach UT took and that they self-disclosed their violations, even though they did so only after newspaper reports exposed them. They were also given credit because most of the infractions involved enrolled student-athletes and were therefore not considered serious violations. They also argued that only one recruit was involved in the infractions so it was no big deal.

So paying enrolled athletes at Texas was okay, but paying enrolled athletes at SMU was bad? Cool, but I couldn't seem to find that distinction in the NCAA manual.

After all those violations, the NCAA penalties were: one-year probation, no sanctions against television, no sanctions against postseason play, and a limitation to no more than twenty scholarships for the 1988-89 academic year. Because the penalties themselves were so mild, the sanction did not even count as a first strike under the Death Penalty statute.

The NCAA even gave Texas significant out-clauses in their findings. Regarding the booster parties, monies, and clothes, the NCAA found that the only violation was that the university "didn't adequately inform the boosters of NCAA rules." Therefore, it was a minor violation. Regarding the erroneous certification of compliance signed by the president, they determined that the president "had no intent to file the erroneous forms" and it was therefore a minor infraction.

They found that monies given were in fact "loans" and that several times had been paid back and were therefore minor. Most other violations were determined to be minor too without the NCAA explaining why. Meals, five years of players' complementary ticket being sold, coaches telling athletes that they could sell their tickets, numerous rides from coaches, cash from coaches, boosters employing recruits, all were considered minor violations.

Even the major violations were excused as "ignorance of the rules." After all, money was only used to "buy a bus ticket home" or "paid a fine the athlete owed the university" or "a bail bond to get out of jail." Boosters were excused for their violations because they were due to "a failure on the part of the university to adequately inform the representatives of the athletics interests of NCAA rules."

In summarizing the infractions and the penalties, the NCAA stated, "these violations in the aggregate constitute a serious infractions case which puts the University of Texas in jeopardy of significantly more serious penalties **should a major violation occur at the university in the future**."

This clause was perhaps the key to the entire NCAA report. Texas was allowed to disclose a limited amount of the total violations that they had committed. This partial confession of previous sins satisfied the NCAA. In return, the NCAA had written into their report that these violations represented a cleaning of house from *all* past violations and that only *future* violations would count against them. They simply had to run a clean program going forward.

In essence, they could shut down their payment system and would not have to fear further investigations or penalties. SMU did not get such a clause in our report. Any and all previous sins, as well as current and future violations would be held against us.

Texas investigated itself and was not forced to disclose the names of the players who sold their tickets. They said that they could not divulge their names without the players' consent. They did disclose that there was a marked difference between what the athletes told the media and what they told the investigators. The school admitted that they did not know "if they reported the truth, but they reported what they were told." The NCAA accepted Texas' story and never interviewed or asked for the names of the athletes involved.

I wish I could be a disinterested observer of how Texas pulled it off, but I can't. I find it fascinating how they co-opted the NCAA enforcement staff. I love how they controlled the timing of it to diminish the effect on recruiting and how they released it during the SMU media circus. I find it incredible they released just enough violations to be accepted and how they adjusted most of the major violations down to minor ones and dismissed the remaining major violations as oversights. Their Head Coach David McWilliams was found guilty of numerous violations and yet he continued as head coach for an additional five years with no NCAA issue.

It helped to have old friend Walter Byers as Executive Director of the NCAA (Byers retired after the Texas verdict). It also helped to have the UT coveting Butch Worley assigned the case (Worley went to work as UT Associate AD under Deloss Dodds the month after the Texas verdict and still works there today).

In short, the violations never happened and the penalties were watered down so much that they had no effect. The way the University of Texas managed their way out of potentially devastating sanctions and painlessly shut down their payment program was simply a work of art.

When a crook pulls off a master heist, even cops have to marvel at the genius of it all. I was impressed. But I guess it was just as George Orwell observed years ago, "All animals are equal, but some animals are more equal than others."

Chapter Forty:
SMU Players after Death

After the Death Penalty was handed down, we had a moment of peace. We didn't know what it all meant or what the future held, but we knew that all the questions would stop and we could get on with our lives.

The locker rooms and coaches' offices were in the old Ownby Stadium located on the southeast corner of SMU's campus. There were still a few department staffers in the building, but it was mostly silent and empty since all of the coaches had been fired the previous December. The day after the penalty was announced, many players cleaned out their lockers. Some took a bit more than their own locker's contents. Anything that wasn't nailed down walked out the front door. I got there late; somebody had already gotten my helmet and gear. Thankfully, they left my shoes.

I didn't know what I was going to do. I had hurt my knee mid-season, but it wasn't career ending and I still had two years I could play. I loved SMU. I had built many friendships and was on track to graduate. I didn't want to leave.

All of us thought of leaving though. Some players knew they could play in the NFL and were focused on the draft in two months. Others needed a last season somewhere else before the 1988 draft. Most of us younger players were interested in transferring away too. But before we could reach out to our former recruiters, the recruiters reached out to us.

SMU made a half attempt to get us to stay but it was too late. Players were elated to be going through the recruiting process again. We were no longer going to be harassed by local media. We were to be courted by national coaches. With the penalty, each of us was released from his contract and could transfer and play without having to sit out a year. For the recruiters, there were fifty-seven proven Division I football players from a top twenty college team that needed a new home. In many cases, a recruiter had lost a player to SMU out of high school and now had a second shot at signing him. They came from around the country. UCLA was there first. Soon, it was crowded.

We didn't have an athletic dorm anymore; Lettermen's Hall had been converted to a regular dorm long before I got there. All of the players lived off campus and few were going to class. There was no one way to find all the players. The recruiters went to SMU's Dedman Center for Lifetime Sports to look for athletes that might be playing basketball. They milled around buildings trying to find us.

Some enterprising coaches figured out that the day after the penalty happened to be the day we got our monthly stipend for room and board. To make rent, we would be coming by Ownby the next day or two to get our checks. And they were waiting for us.

As we trickled in, we walked through the coaches and heard their pitches. "What's your name son?" They had lists. They knew who they wanted. All they had to do was figure out who you were. A lot of the players had a blast. After months and even years of negative stories, negative comments, and a generally negative atmosphere, it was nice to see some positive energy. The program was dead but we weren't. It was recruiting season again when all was possible. There were trips to take, promises to be made, and dreams that could be chased.

I watched it all and was conflicted. I was recruited by a number of schools but they weren't my schools. I was from Colorado. I had grown up a Big Eight and WAC guy watching Colorado, BYU, and Wyoming. I had gotten excited about aerial shootouts between Jim McMahon's BYU and a scrappy Air Force Academy. I didn't know or like the other schools in the SWC or in the south, just SMU.

So here were all these schools that I would never have played for out of high school recruiting me now after three years at SMU. It didn't compute. To the guys who grew up in Texas and followed the SWC or the SEC I got it. But for me, the only exposure I had to those schools was as teams to beat, not as teams to join.

One by one players started dropping. First up were Dave Richards and Ben Hummel to UCLA. They were on the quarter system so they could enroll for the spring quarter…it was time to go…now. Most other guys were looking at schools on the semester system and it was too late to enroll and play spring ball. Summer would have to do. But if they were transferring, why go to class? So they took their trips, they made their commitments, and then they disappeared from campus.

We could still work out in the football weight room. It was pretty quiet and you didn't have to wait to get on a machine. A handful of guys that couldn't transfer until the fall continued to work out on their own schedule. We were not teammates anymore. We were just acquaintances who had bled together and were now moving on to our own individual futures. It was sad. All the history, all the memories, all the tradition, went out the door with all the players as they moved on to their new teams. Most of them never looked back. They were forced to commit to a new coach and a new team.

Some found great success like Derrick Reed and Jeffrey Jacobs who got to go to the Rose Bowl with Michigan State and beat USC to finish #8 in the nation. Others like Ben Hummel and David Richards got to go back to the Aloha

Bowl in Hawaii but this time as Bruins. Many went on to the NFL with alma maters of LSU, UCLA, and Houston as their final stop before the draft. They were not listed from SMU.

David Berst still wanted the names of the three paid players with eligibility. But since the names of the players remained anonymous, the NCAA could only guess. He did warn other schools that if the players were discovered, they would be declared ineligible and games they played in would be forfeited. Many schools took the position that the only way to ensure that they didn't take one of the three unnamed players was to take none of the players.

I remember deciding that I would not transfer to a lesser school just to play football. I remember that nobody from the NCAA called or counseled us as to what we should do during those difficult days. I remember being alone. I looked at and ranked the schools that I would transfer to. I calculated the number of hours I would lose by transferring. And then I decided that I would only go through the difficulties of transferring if I could get a better deal. I figured if I could get as good or better an education and continue playing football, then I would try playing somewhere else.

I wanted a private school in a great location with a great football program. For three years, I had that. I wasn't giving it up. The only schools that seemed a fit for me were USC, Stanford, and maybe Miami. Of the three, Stanford was the most exciting. I was born in northern California and my father's family lived there. Miami and USC were facing the same NCAA investigations and violations SMU faced, so they were not good options. Stanford became the only school that I felt was worth the disruption of leaving SMU. Since they didn't come to our campus to recruit us, I called them.

I talked to the recruiting coach. He was very polite. He slowly told me that Stanford had made a conscious choice to not come to the SMU campus and recruit our released players. I told him I had the grades and I would come out there on my own nickel. I offered to send him film. Then he told me,

"Dave, don't take this the wrong way, but Stanford is not interested in any players from SMU. The taint that the Death Penalty has put on all of you is not something Stanford wants on its campus." After I caught my breath, I thanked him and hung up.

So there it was. *The taint.* I did nothing wrong and yet I was tainted. The only other school that I thought was worth the academic disruption of transferring to play football didn't want me. So I gave up on football and I turned my attention back to SMU and getting a degree.

This was not so easy and deciding to stay was not without consequences. The NCAA scandal had rocked the SMU campus. The general student body was in revolt. There were protests every day. Many professors attempted to put down and blame the few of us former players still in class. We were evil. We were the cause of diminished academic prestige. We had targets on our backs.

Normally a football player takes twelve hours during the fall season and then tries to catch up during spring semester or summer break. The spring of 1987 I enrolled in fifteen hours of regular classes and one hour of a required PE class. By late March, I was failing all of them. I didn't care. I was sick of it. I was labeled as one of the reasons SMU was in such chaos and I stopped going to class.

Not everyone was against us. A number of us were ATOs and I remember our fraternity brothers stepping up. The guys that we had gone through pledgeship, Hell Week, and numerous social events, recognized that we weren't to blame and they protected us. We had a safe place to go where no one would accuse us of being crooks. Other players in other fraternities were also protected. The former players who were not fraternity guys were on their own.

Out of all this, a professor of English named Bonnie Wheeler reached out to me. She was a tough teacher and not particularly gentle on football players. In fact, I remember her being pretty tough on me. So when she called me to her office and asked me what was going on, I was surprised. I told her I was failing every class and that I didn't want to be around campus with all the animosity. She said that my goal should be to survive that semester and regroup for the fall when things might be clearer. She told me if I failed that semester, SMU could kick me out and I would lose football and my college degree. We went over my class schedule and she advised me to drop every class that I was destined to fail, and keep those few I could pass. I kept two electives and my PE class for a total of seven hours. I didn't fail out of school that semester, and I thank Bonnie for that.

Professor Wheeler was right. In the fall things were clearer and it did get better. So I re-enrolled, went to class, and I tried to put it all behind me. I pretended like nothing had happened. Nothing at all.

SPECIAL REPORT:

SMU BEYOND THE DEATH PENALTY

ERIN POWERS Staff SUN 07/12/1987 HOUSTON CHRONICLE, Section Sports, Page 18, 2 STAR Edition

DALLAS - Dave Blewett saw some of his SMU teammates playing the recruiting game all over again when the Southwest Conference approved their immediate transfers elsewhere. He knew his decision to stay was the right one.

Nearly 60 players were immediately eligible to play at other schools after the NCAA imposed its so-called "death penalty." But Blewett, now a junior, chose to continue his studies despite the many chances to leave.

Still somewhat bitter about the downfall of the program, Blewett was equally disgusted with the displays of greed and deceit he saw in other recruiters, many of whom were nearly camping on the campus.

Blewett chose to avoid potential problems, forsaking several scholarship offers from Big Eight and WAC schools.

He seriously considered only Duke, California and Stanford, none of which had scholarships as late as he became available. So the transition into the "mainstream" was on.

Unlike in 1985, when a point-shaving scandal caused Tulane to eliminate its basketball program and the scholarships that accompanied it, SMU committed itself to an expensive project - which could cost as much as $600,000 - and offered former players a variety of options.

Blewett, of Englewood, Colo., took one to continue his education at SMU.

"This school has a lot more going for it than athletics," says Blewett, a real estate-finance major. "People in the business world respect a degree from SMU. And this city is good for what I want to end up doing."

By next year, he will probably have two degrees. The university will also pay for a year of graduate school if he qualifies. Blewett expects to.

"There was a lot of mixed reaction when I chose to stay at SMU, even in my family. But this is far better for my long-term future."

SMU faculty representative Lonnie Kliever says the school chose to honor the scholarship commitments out of a moral obligation.

"Nowhere was it written that they had to do it," Blewett says. "I think they tried to right some of the wrongs."

Listed in last year's game program as 6 feet 3 and 270 pounds, Blewett is considerably lighter now, having lost 40 pounds since February through dieting.

"There's no sense in weighing that much anymore. I can't eat three, four or five sandwiches at a time now. I want to slim down. Football at SMU is gone," he says.

Chapter Forty-One:
SMU Community after Death

In the immediate aftermath of the Death Penalty, the school was in turmoil. In fact, turmoil isn't a strong enough word. The school was in an existential crisis. The Board of Governors was hopelessly compromised. The Board of Trustees was leaderless. The faculty was in open revolt with most wanting athletics off campus altogether. Students were also in revolt from the perceived drop in prestige of their degrees.

Now that the penalty was assessed and the players penalized, there was nothing of interest for the media to report about the team. So their glare moved off of us players and on to the leaders of the school.

As stated in the NCAA report and emphasized by SMU officials, the names of staff members and student-athletes would not be made public. The violations were specifically tied to "certain key athletics department staff" and one "key booster" who agreed that promises made to student-athletes prior to the 1984-85 academic year when they were recruited, would continue to be fulfilled.

David Berst was still chasing us. He said that further sanctions could be imposed if it were proved that high-ranking SMU officials were guilty of hitherto undiscovered violations. But later, noting that the school's dormant football program wouldn't be resumed until 1989 at the earliest, Berst said, "To be honest, I don't know what else can be done to SMU."

A week after the NCAA report, Bob Hitch was outed as knowing all about the payment scheme. But he was already gone. That same week, Governor Bill Clements was dogged by reporters until he came clean. On March 2, he admitted that he and some other members of the Board of Governors had approved the continuation of the improper payments as a "moral obligation" and part of a "winding down" process. But he had already been re-elected as Texas Governor and resigned from the SMU Board of Governors. He was untouchable.

On March 21, the Board of Governors was abolished by the Board of Trustees. Then the thirty-one members of that Board resigned to make way for a new generation of leaders.

Bodies were flying everywhere as a new guard moved in motivated to clean house and rebuild in a new way. The idea was to get control and then knock athletics down to a lower place within the school. The to-be-determined president and faculty would be running things now.

The school debated dropping football all together or coming back as a Division III school without scholarships. An SMU committee released a divided report that recommended staying Division I but we would do it with our hands tied behind our backs. We eliminated "special admissions" for athletes and minimum academic standards were raised to a 2.0 GPA and 900 SAT score (200 points higher than NCAA standards). Between 1980 and 1984 almost half of our football team had been special admits (forty-eight players). Regardless of the debate, those decisions made us a de facto Division III school.

During those chaotic years in the aftermath of the penalty, SMU did not have many friends. If the NCAA or our Southwest Conference rivals had any remorse for what they did or for how far they had gone, they didn't show it. The

Dallas community moved on, and we were left to our tragic end.

SMU's future came down to a small group of people who loved the school and were willing to do the hard work to bring it back. Thankfully, there were enough benefactors who supported the school and recognized that it was imperative to not give up. The new trustees, particularly Ray Hunt, hired Dr. Kenneth Pye from Duke University as our new president. Many people believe that was a mistake in terms of athletics, as he was not a supporter and made the rebuilding task more difficult. He didn't want to fund sports, he didn't want academic waivers for athletes, and he didn't want sports emphasized as it had been. There is no doubt he was responsible for preventing a rapid rise back to football prominence.

But in his defense, Dr. Pye was hired to manage a school deep in crisis. I can envision the faculty and student body erupting if we immediately re-emphasized a big time football program. Too many people were absolutely against going back to where we had been. In fact, it was a closely run thing that we even had football again when we were allowed to start up. Perhaps Dr. Pye was able to convince enough of the faculty and administration that he was on their side, and in that role he gave athletics enough room to survive. Perhaps he really didn't like athletics at the college level. Either way, there is no doubt that President Pye's integrity and strength allowed SMU to weather the internal challenges we faced and then to start to solve those challenges.

There is also no doubt that the elimination of special admits prevented SMU from recruiting at the highest levels. We decided to stay and compete in the Southwest Conference with a different caliber of athlete than that of our competition. Those first few years in 1989 through the end of the Southwest Conference in 1995 when we were attempting to rebuild, were crucial. Our win-loss record should have been terrible for a few years, but by year three or so we could have had the talent and the depth to win and then begin to thrive again. It was difficult enough starting over with a new team, but without the special admits we just didn't have key players that would have made the difference between a winning and a losing season.

And what could we have done to anticipate the dissolution of the Southwest Conference? If we recruited well and won some games and remained in a top tier conference, we could have flipped the switch and rebuilt the program whenever we chose. We could have offered what SMU always offered: great academics, a dynamic student body, a wealth of alumni and community resources, the opportunity to play the best football teams in the country, vie for conference and national championships, and the excitement of being in the heart of one of the most vibrant big cities in the nation Dallas, Texas.

For SMU, once the Southwest Conference dissolved we could still offer the academics and the opportunities of the SMU community, but the best high school players would have to go to other programs to have a chance at big time football. Some great players did come to SMU after the Death Penalty, but slowly our reputation began to fade. Then our rivals gladly talked of our program in the past. And finally, our rivals left us behind.

Chapter Forty-Two:
It Wasn't Right

I was part of one of the best football programs in the history of college football. We had the best players, we had the best coaches, and we won the most games. Many would say that we paid for all that.

Well, I was there and that's been exaggerated beyond belief. I didn't get paid. My buddies didn't get paid. Sure, we paid some players a bonus if they came to SMU through the early 1980's, but we didn't pay the overwhelming majority of our players. A handful of our poorer players continued to be given monthly stipends into the mid 1980's to help with expenses. We operated in a manner consistent with other top-flight programs of that era.

Up until 1974, SMU football was no different than any other program in the country. We experienced periods of greatness and then mediocrity and then greatness again. We were penalized for two minor violations that occurred during the previous twenty years. When the NCAA made their great push in the mid 1970's to get "institutional control" over athletics, SMU led the way.

Our President Hardin was a believer that presidents should control athletics. He fired Coach Hayden Fry for breaking the rules and then turned in his replacement to the

NCAA when he broke the rules too. The resulting turmoil led to Hardin's termination. His termination led the NCAA to come after us again the following year.

In 1976 new Coach Ron Meyer arrived and began the big drive to compete for and sign the best athletes in the state. The SWC was already out of control. In 1975, longtime friends Darrell Royal of Texas, Frank Broyles of Arkansas, and Walter Byers of the NCAA met privately in Dallas to discuss the out-of-control cheating in the conference. The coaches felt the old arrangements were breaking down and smaller schools were challenging their positions. Byers pledged to help them stem the tide. A year later both coaches retired blaming the new environment.

We really had only two chances to avoid the Death Penalty. The easiest was if we never set up the payment scheme in the first place. SMU would have struggled while our rivals continued to sign better recruits with the help of their payment schemes. In that situation, the NCAA could not have used us as their fall guy.

The second chance was when we hired Donald Shields as president in October 1980. He was informed that we paid some of our players and he wanted it stopped, but he made no move to stop it. Every year he was required to sign the President's Statement that our school was following all NCAA rules. He knowingly signed those false statements each year and sent them to the NCAA. His excuse was that members of the Board of Governors told him to go "run the school and leave athletics to them." Sorry, the Board of Governors did not have to sign the annual contract with the NCAA like he did.

Coach Collins and AD Hitch had clauses in their employment contracts specifying that they comply with NCAA rules, but they were employees of and contracted with SMU and therefore of Shields. Shields had three years where he could have shut the scheme down without triggering the destruction of our team. It would have been difficult and it would have meant fighting with some powerful SMU board members. Nonetheless, Shields was responsible and chose not to act. By 1983 it was too late.

Once the NCAA got to use their new weapon on us, they had a scalp to carry around and show the sports world they were in charge. They expected members to take heed and start following the rules. But athletic programs just became more careful as they continued to break the rules. More money poured into college football and more scandals erupted. SMU's example was all for naught.

Eventually the NCAA and Walter Byers accepted defeat. In his 1995 book *Unsportsmanlike Conduct*, Byers reversed his entire life's work. He admitted the NCAA "lost the battle to protect the concept of amateurism," that college athletes are "exploited in the system he constructed," and that his own over-regulated NCAA rule book "restricts an athlete's rights to gain economic freedom."

Apparently the head of the NCAA, the guy who wrote the rule book and chased all the rule breakers, eventually gave up and then said "never mind." Selfishly, it would have been nice for SMU if Byers had his epiphany and conversion in the mid-eighties instead of the mid-nineties. But, SMU didn't seem to catch many lucky breaks back then.

David Stanley couldn't catch a break either. After the Death Penalty, he tried to play football in the Canadian leagues and then ended up back home in Angleton, Texas. I couldn't find out much about him except that he never recovered from turning on SMU. It seems it was the high point and low point of his life. Just like Stopperich, he argued that SMU's downfall wasn't his fault. Tragically, he also died of an overdose in 2005 just as Stopperich did in 1995.

Thinking back on all that happened, I am hard pressed to see how SMU could have handled the endgame differently. The Ron Meyer era of paying recruits had ended. The leftover era of paying existing players was winding down. The Stopperich probation in 1985 probably could have been avoided if SMU had released him from his Letter of Intent.

The Stanley 1986 disclosures that resulted in the Death Penalty probably could have been avoided too. But even without Stanley, the NCAA would have kept chasing us until they came up with something else.

I don't see how NCAA sanctions and personal grudges gave SMU any viable option. Self-report? Cover up? Continue to pay? Shut it down? Death Penalty in all cases.

Its twenty-five years later and I still don't understand that penalty. Not one guilty person was penalized in any way under the Death Penalty while us seventy-one innocent players were collectively grouped together, branded with a scarlet letter "C" for cheating, and penalized for things done by individuals long gone. It wasn't right.

Chapter Forty-Three:
Chasing the NCAA

The paralegal walked me through a confusing maze of halls to a large conference room where my lawyer, John Wander, stood gazing at reams of paper scattered along an onyx table that went on forever. As I got closer, I saw the Jerry Tarkanian case highlighted and filled with notes. There was the CFA case and numerous others cases involving the NCAA and college sports. Clearly, he had been doing a lot of work. I thanked God we were friends.

We began going over everything and checking different angles to pursue litigation. The first hurdle I had to get over was standing. Typically, only a member university or named individual in an infractions report has the standing to pursue the NCAA. Neither my name nor any other member of the SMU football team was mentioned in the 1987 report. But the spirit of the rule was that named and penalized individuals could appeal because they were the ones harmed. In that report, our entire team was named and harmed. As a member of that group, I felt I had standing. Wander agreed. He believed we could win that issue. It would allow us to get into court. Then we had to have a reason to stay.

The next hurdle was the statute of limitations. My ability to sue the NCAA in court for how they treated me and the rest of my innocent teammates in 1987 had long expired. Yet, there was no statute of limitations on filing an appeal with the NCAA Appeals Committee.

What if I appealed the Death Penalty to the NCAA? They regularly vacated records and even national championships when they turned up old violations. Why not vacate the penalty if we turned up old violations by the NCAA?

My lawyer said the NCAA was nothing but lawyers who protected their "system." He said they would fight, and then he asked if I was prepared.

I responded, "Sometimes just picking a fight is winning, regardless of the outcome." I kept thinking back to the movie *Animal House*. The fraternity guys of Delta Tau Chi were on "Double Secret Probation" throughout the movie. When they screwed up again, Dean Wormer leaped at the opportunity to expel the Delta's and shut down their fraternity house.

At this point the guys had lost and Dean Wormer had won. John "Bluto" Belushi gets up and makes one of the all-time great speeches. He says…"it ain't over until *we* say it's over…that it wasn't over when the 'Germans' bombed Pearl Harbor," and other enlightened observations one could expect from a seventh year student with a "zero-point-zero" GPA. His fraternity brothers rally to make one final gesture, no matter that it was already a lost cause. "Sometimes you just have to do something." They then go on to destroy the homecoming parade.

I wasn't suggesting anything that pointless or destructive, but I was suggesting that sometimes you fight back even if you are destined to lose. Some of the greatest battles of all time were destined for certain defeat and yet are remembered today as important. The 300 of Sparta, The Alamo, and the Polish Cavalry charging Hitler's tanks in WWII came to mind.

Here I am twenty-five years after the penalty and I feel like we never even tried to fight back. I don't like that feeling. It's wrong. So I told my lawyer I wanted to pick a fight with the NCAA and specifically with the corrupt David Berst.

When I finished explaining my commitment to him, he asked me what the violations would be. I told him I felt the NCAA violated its own Rules of Procedure to convict us. Yes, it was a technicality, but I didn't care. Rules were rules. If we had to follow them, so should they.

I could have gone back and tried to build a case that the NCAA specifically targeted us the decade leading up to the Death Penalty but I decided to concentrate on the last investigation

I focused on the David Stanley allegations that led to the Death Penalty and was the culmination of the NCAA's pursuit. That case began October 22, 1986 and concluded February 25, 1987. I got a copy of the NCAA manual from 2011 and the specific Rules of Procedure the NCAA had to adhere to in an investigation. Wander argued I needed the manual from 1986 and got me a copy. There wasn't much of a difference between the two manuals. They rewrote and moved the chapters around, but substantively the rules for them hadn't changed much. We listed them out on the white board.

The first series of rules they broke related to how the Stanley investigation began and the NCAA's obligations. According to Section 2-b and 2-c of the 1986 NCAA manual "the investigative staff, so far as practicable, shall make a thorough investigation of all charges that are received from responsible sources and are reasonably substantial. The investigative staff may initiate an investigation on its own motion when it has reasonable cause to believe that a member is or has been in violation. The investigative staff may conduct a *preliminary inquiry* for a reasonable period of time to determine whether there is adequate evidence to warrant an official inquiry; and in conducting this inquiry, the services of a field investigator may be used."

Berst broke rule 2-b by sending a field investigator before he opened an official preliminary inquiry. He was conducting a secret investigation against the rules.

Berst was on record stating that "we don't have the luxury of starting an investigation because someone is suspicious." But David Stanley did not call the NCAA to turn himself in and the NCAA had no reasonable cause to believe we were in violation. There were no media reports before the NCAA dispatched Worley.

If Berst was investigating us he had to notify us. Sections 2-b and 12-a-2 state "if the enforcement staff decides information has been developed to indicate that violations of the Association's governing legislation may have occurred that will require further in-person investigation, they shall submit letters to notify member institutions of preliminary inquiries into their athletics policies and practices. Such a letter shall advise the institution that the preliminary inquiry will entail the use of a field investigator."

Berst broke rule 12-a-2 by conducting an investigation without notifying SMU and never sent the Preliminary Letter of Inquiry before or after Worley's interview.

If the director for enforcement determined that an allegation or complaint warranted an official inquiry, Section 3-b says he "shall determine its scope and thrust and direct another Official Letter of Inquiry to the chief executive officer of the member involved." We didn't get that letter either.

Part of their secret investigation was the selective leaking of confidential information. Berst had long since leaked Stanley to WFAA's Sparks. He also discussed the ongoing case with the media. Sections 11 and 12-a-15 state the "enforcement staff shall not confirm or deny the existence of an infractions case prior to complete resolution of the case through normal NCAA enforcement procedures. The Committee on Infractions and the Council shall treat all cases before them as confidential."

Yet in November 1986, Berst repeatedly said; "if the allegations against SMU are proved—and he indicated that SMU would be investigated further—then the school could become the first death-penalty victim." He wasn't allowed to make any public comments until the conclusion of the case. But he did and he corrupted the process.

Apparently, the NCAA was free to open and conduct an investigation, interview witnesses, and leak confidential information to media sources without having to follow their own Rules of Procedure. I disagreed.

The NCAA has an appeals process. It was designed to set aside errors arrived at by the Infractions Committee. There were three valid ways to appeal: if the committee's findings were contrary to the evidence presented, if the findings did not constitute violations of the rules, or if there was a prejudicial error by the enforcement staff in the procedures that were followed in processing a case.

The NCAA enforcement staff clearly broke their own rules in pursuing David Stanley. It is conceivable that if they had not broken their rules, David Stanley's allegations would never have spawned the media frenzy that led to the SMU self-disclosures. The Infractions Committee might never have even seen the case, and we would not have received the Death Penalty.

Yes, it was a technicality and we were guilty of the violations in the report. But if they didn't want appeals based on procedural errors on the part of NCAA staff, they shouldn't have included those appeals in their manual. Their errors were legitimate grounds to appeal.

I told my attorney that was what I wanted to do; I wanted to file an appeal with the NCAA to overturn the 1987 Death Penalty based on prejudicial errors by David Berst and his enforcement staff in their investigation of SMU.

Chapter Forty-Four:
Above the Law?

I sat there with Wander discussing my options. The NCAA had clearly broken its own rules in pursuing SMU. The NCAA also fashioned and used a penalty that punished innocent players not affiliated with the violations. Then the NCAA structured itself as untouchable and above the law.

Why was it the NCAA called the simplest things infractions, while the employees of the non-profit and tax exempt NCAA had company cars, gold-plated expense accounts, multiple six-figure salaries, and a reserve slush fund amounting to billions of dollars. How did a voluntary organization initially set up to prevent injuries and promote standardized rules of play become the dictatorial government of the schools that made up its membership?

How did they come to promote, own, and then control all the revenues from the billion dollar NCAA March Madness basketball tournament? How did they get the power to dictate a school's mascot, or control and profit from the likenesses of all former athletes without compensating the actual athletes? And worst of all, how did they establish authority over individual athletes like me without giving us the right to defend ourselves?

In my case, they had the power to penalize me and the rest of my teammates when even *they* acknowledged we had not broken any of their rules. They had the power to make us quit football or transfer to different schools against our wishes. Then they told us that since they had given us the choice, we were actually in control of the situation. It was similar to the kings of old allowing a condemned man to choose which part of his body would be chopped off to satisfy the request for a "pound of flesh." I suppose we should have thanked them.

And yet if we were to complain, they would not deign to grant us a hearing. They are a feudal system in modern America. The only rights we subjects have are the rights our schools are able to secure on our behalf. And of course as in feudal times, the more powerful your Lord, the more rights you have as a serf. In this modern incarnation of feudalism, the larger and more politically connected schools are the ones with more rights.

The NCAA regularly stated that since they were not a legally controlling entity, they were not obligated to offer due process rights to members or athletes. The following quote came to mind as I understood more about their structure:

It is convenient to have a system of laws where everyone is a criminal.

Well, it *was* convenient for the NCAA to have a system where all schools could be reasonably expected to be breaking some obscure bylaw in some forgotten chapter of their manual. For the NCAA to decide to look around a school was for the NCAA to find that school guilty of something.

In this way, evidence in an investigation was not the determining factor for sanctions, the decision to look around was. And David Berst was the sole decider of who was chosen. Over and over he chose SMU whether allegations were phoned in to the NCAA or created by him. SMU was his designated whipping boy.

How else could he argue that we were the worst? He could say we paid out a lot of money. We paid $61,000 to our players. But others paid their players more: TCU ($400,000), Miami ($620,000), UCLA (over $1 million), Oklahoma ($500,000) and the list goes on. The amount of money in the SMU scandal is a pittance compared to numerous other scandals.

He could say our violations were structural and covered numerous years (1983-86) or back to 1979 if you really want to stretch. But others were as long or longer: UCLA (a decade or more), Texas (ten years of illicit ticket selling), and Miami (1989-94).

He could say that the number of players involved set us apart. We had thirteen admitted players involved, but others had more: Miami (over 200 athletes), Texas (over 100 athletes), and Oklahoma State (29 athletes).

He could say that our scandal reached the highest levels of governance at SMU, including a former Governor of the state of Texas. But none of those revelations came out until *after* the Death Penalty was assessed.

No, the sole reason we were considered the worst was the number of times the NCAA investigated us. Since 1974, all five of our investigations were ordered by David Berst. Of those five: 1974 was self-reported, 1975 was generated internally at the NCAA by Berst himself, 1981 and 1983 were in response to UT and other Southwest Conference schools reporting us, and 1987 was also generated internally at the NCAA by Berst.

"Dave. Dave! Are you with me?" My lawyer was snapping his fingers in front of my face.

"Yeah, I'm with you. I was just thinking about the entire situation, trying to appeal the penalty and my lost eligibility."

"Dave, with all the work you've done and the bullets we have, there is a way...are you sure you want to do this?"

"Yeah, I'm sure...what do we do now?"

He told me that first of all I needed the media on my side. There were too many instances of the NCAA simply swatting away players, coaches, boosters, and even schools who challenged them. Nobody had been able to beat them except Jerry Tarkanian of UNLV. He spent over a decade and untold amounts in legal fees chasing the NCAA before he finally won and secured his $2.5mm settlement.

He only won because of his tenaciousness. Most others that went after the NCAA gave up after a few years of NCAA stonewalling and unaffordable legal fees.

For the NCAA it was easy. They were nothing but a bunch of lawyers. It cost them nothing to drag things out.

My lawyer knew all that. He said the only strategy that would work for me was to generate enough media interest for the NCAA to have to respond to questions from them about my story. He said they would never respond to just me.

So the question became, how could I get the media to take an interest in my story? How could I get them to help me in my quest to challenge the NCAA for breaking their bylaws in the pursuit of SMU?

I told my lawyer I was going to write a book about what really happened…and then the media would have to help me.

Wander laughed and made me a bet. He told me that if I wrote a book and it made the New York Times Bestseller List, he would file the appeal pro bono and happily help me overturn the Death Penalty.

I accepted the bet.

As I walked out of his office confident in overcoming this new hurdle, I was pretty sure I could hear him chuckling softly. It was a safe bet for him. There was no possible way I would write a book or make that list.

Maybe he was right, but I had come this far. How hard could it be? It was just a book…people wrote them every day. Why not me?

Chapter Forty-Five:
The NCAA Today

The central organizing principle of the NCAA was to protect amateurism in college athletics and they have failed. Too much money flows into the schools, conferences, television networks, coaches, and the NCAA for anybody to honestly believe college football is an amateur sport. The only thing amateur is the non-paid athlete laboring in the for-profit system. The NCAA knows this.

After they sanctioned SMU in 1987, the NCAA recognized that the main reason players were continuing to be paid was that the poorest athletes had no means of supporting themselves during college. A scholarship did not cover all the expenses of attending college. The NCAA determined that the difference between scholarship grants and the true cost of college is around $3000 per year. That's pretty close to the payment amounts that resulted in SMU's penalty.

Think about that for a minute. The NCAA knew then and knows today that their own rules make it extremely difficult for the poor and increasingly black athletes to cover their living expenses. And yet they target anybody that attempts to make up that shortfall.

Federal Pell Grants were established to help poor students cover the costs of college. The NCAA initially allowed poor athletes to apply for the $2,400 annual grants yet let them keep only a portion of it. In 1993 the NCAA amended its policy to allow the full Pell Grant to be given to poor athletes above and beyond an athletic scholarship. Today, the amount authorized for Pell Grants is around $5,000 and the athletes are allowed to keep it all.

These funds are being raided to supplement scholarship athletes at the expense of poor kids who really need the grants. Approximately 20% of Big Ten scholarship football players and as many as 60% of Southeast Conference players receive an average of $4500 per year in Pell Grants beyond their scholarships. The NCAA justifies these extra payments from the Federal government because of the shortfall that they calculated.

In 2012 the NCAA Board of Directors approved a $2,000 annual payment above and beyond Pell Grants and scholarships to cover the full cost of college. It was voted down by the membership. But it needs to be noted that the enforcement guys, the NCAA, wanted to pay extra monies to athletes against the wishes of the colleges themselves.

What? The NCAA is approving extra payments now?

The NCAA even has a Special Assistance Fund to help cover the cost of things like medical expenses (SMU got in trouble for paying for David Stanley's 1985 drug treatment program), and trips home (like the trips home that caused the probation SMU received in 1964).

All these payments and the amounts fascinate me. The NCAA bends over backwards to prevent some entities from giving money to players and then they promote others. The difference is school and government money is good money while booster money is bad, I guess.

But then came the University of Miami. Between 1989 and 1994 they fraudulently obtained over $624,000 in Pell Grants and improper financial aid monies for over 200 different athletes. That did get them put on a light probation.

Apparently some government money was good and other government money was bad. It was all so confusing.

What's going on is the NCAA is trying to pay college athletes a wage without having the money qualify as wages and they can't figure out how to do it. The minute these attempts to pay players become qualified as wages, the NCAA and college football as we know it are done. Worker's compensation laws would kick in along with federal withholding tax, social security, disability and of course employment laws in each state. But the big kicker is that the players would be qualified as professional football employees and then we would see how much the market would pay for their talents.

After the U.S. Supreme Court decision and football television deregulation, television revenues went to the individual conferences and teams. In need of revenue, the schools decided they needed to play more regular season games. The best way to do that was to expand the conferences to super conferences and add conference championships. The NCAA stood largely on the sidelines irrelevant to the negotiations.

Over time, the CFA gave way to the Bowl Championship Series (BCS) which included all the biggest football schools this time. The BCS has succeeded in segregating the largest schools' conferences away from the smaller schools and conferences. In 2006 the BCS system generated $125.9 million. The big six conferences split $118.9 million, the other five conferences received $5.2 million, and the smaller I-AA schools received $1.8 million. Those numbers didn't include conference television contracts which are even more heavily weighted towards the big time conferences.

Because of this disparity, the big time schools are pulling further and further away from all the non-BCS schools. The top seventy-five or so football-playing programs have fresh motivation to explore breaking away and forming their own governing body again. The old CFA and now the BCS has shown the way forward without the NCAA as their regulatory authority.

The NCAA views a football playoff system as a mortal threat to their existence. If schools could put together such a system without the NCAA's assistance, then perhaps the March Madness basketball tournament doesn't need the NCAA either. If schools could cut out the NCAA as middle man they could share the $1 billion payout themselves.

The NCAA funds 78% of its operations from that tournament. Without that money they would be reduced to a rule book without power. They would be an organization without the means to enforce any of its edicts.

Because of these developments, the old punishments of TV bans and death penalties are gone. There is too much money involved and member institutions would fight back. New punishments are either symbolic slaps or they fall on players, street agents, and any other weak links they can target. They cannot afford to make enemies of members who just might vote the NCAA out of existence.

The bottom line is that the frauds that the NCAA have rested on are coming back to bite them. There is no such thing as a student-athlete. They are either students or they are athletes and one must be chosen. Institutions have responsibilities for athletes that are injured while "earning" their scholarship on the field. The NCAA has no real authority to impose penalties on athletes who they say have no standing with them. These same athletes must have the same due process protections every citizen has when dealing with any other institution. And finally, these athletes must be paid to reflect the economic benefit they provide to the marketplace.

Ramogi Huma, a former linebacker at UCLA and the founder of the National College Players Association, says they should "open up the market to the players on commercial revenue. You can have the open market or the black market. The NCAA has chosen the black market. They'll put up with the scandals along the way...but at some point it becomes ridiculous. We're teetering on that point right now." He thinks that paying athletes a modest amount - a few thousand dollars a year - would lessen the temptation to break NCAA rules by taking cash from boosters, agents and anyone else willing to give it. Opponents of pay-for-play argue that it would only provide plausible deniability for even more brazen player buying.

The crux of the problem is that superstar athletes are in financial prison while they are in college. Without financial help from parents, they are the poorest kids on campus. So some cheat and do stupid things to make a few bucks while coaches who very well know how broke these kids are, look the other way.

This is the system the NCAA has set up.

Chapter Forty-Six:
Answering Amanda

As I revisited Amanda's fateful question, I was forced to revisit all my memories and feelings about the SMU Scandal. I couldn't completely answer her when she asked, but I can today…

Dear Amanda,

It's hard not to consider what might have been if the NCAA hadn't targeted SMU and me for termination. I was not a great football player, but I would have had a couple more years of getting stronger and better. I might not have been drafted into the NFL, but I know I would have tried to play. Most likely I would have been cut, and I can accept that. It's also possible that I would have hurt my knee again or much worse had I continued playing. But I would have gone as far as my abilities allowed and that is how it should have ended.

I was forced to get more serious about my future while I still had two years in college. I studied harder and didn't just graduate, I graduated with two degrees. That would have been much more difficult if I had played football those last two years. I was able to get a good job out of college and start my life. That allowed me to build a career, meet your mother, and then build the wonderful family that I adore, including you.

When you asked, "did I do anything wrong when I played football at SMU?" I realized that I needed an answer for you and that I never fully understood what happened back then. They were really opposite sides of the same coin. Did I do anything wrong and what really happened? We both deserved an answer.

Strange that it took so long to bubble up. But here it is, staring at me...asking me other questions, challenging me. Was it okay to be damaged by a faceless bureaucracy and not fight back? Did I wait too long?

I decided it was not okay to be harmed without fighting back and that there is no time limit to do so. I survived a tough time without any support back then but here I am, twenty-five years later to set the record straight.

I tried to play football again. I figured it would help me answer your question. I thought I could show you that I was a football player and that it was a positive thing. I had visions of suiting up, washing away all the bad old memories, and creating good fresh memories.

I didn't get to play again, but I did get motivated to write a book. In that book I tried to answer everything that happened back then and also tell you about me.

The information I learned motivated me to pursue the NCAA in order to overturn their unfair penalty and fight them.

College football experienced great turmoil as television became more important. Tremendous money started pouring in for the benefit of everyone but the players. In order to deny players that money, the NCAA had to create and protect the concept of amateurism. But money found its way to the players anyway.

While I was at SMU, some players were paid an allowance to cover their living expenses. I was not one of them.

My parents were able to send me a few hundred dollars a month to cover those living expenses, but the poorer athletes from rougher neighborhoods had no such resources to fall back on. They were paid by associates of the SMU community the same as my parents paid me.

The NCAA investigated SMU seven times over a thirty-year period and five of those investigations were started by David Berst. This same David Berst was shown to have a personal bias against SMU and noted he could find any school guilty if he simply opened an investigation. That was wrong.

The NCAA chose to repeatedly target SMU to make an example of us for the rest of the association. In doing so, they broke their own rules. That was wrong.

The NCAA was tasked with protecting and helping us players and somehow along the way forgot that. When they penalized us innocent players, they never advised or helped us through their disruptions. That was wrong.

I did play on that targeted and trapped 1987 SMU football team. I know what happened now, and I'm comfortable answering your question.

"No baby I didn't do anything wrong, but that doesn't mean wrong wasn't done."

Love, Dad

Epilogue:
Forgiveness and Bishop's Report

I Forgive Them

I forgive Walter Byers, the NCAA Executive Director, for nursing a grudge against SMU All-American Jimmy Kitts when Byers was a nineteen-year-old college football hopeful. I forgive him for his bias towards large state schools at the expense of smaller private institutions. I forgive him for stacking his committees with other biased and like-minded members who did his bidding.

I forgive David Berst for compromising his ethics in trying to please his boss, Walter Byers. I forgive him for leaking private NCAA information to his media sources and bypassing his Rules of Procedure. I forgive him for his arrogance towards anybody who stood up to him or the NCAA. I forgive him for his embellishments and his lies in the pursuit of SMU.

I forgive Deloss Dodds, AD at UT, who inherited an athletic department in decline and made the decision to use his personal relationships at the NCAA and the NCAA machinery itself to take out a rival football program. I forgive him for turning in SMU for breaking the same rules he was breaking. For him, it was business.

I forgive John Sparks, WFAA producer and UT football booster, who was given the lead on David Stanley from the biased NCAA and used it to further his career. I forgive him for breaking the Journalistic Code of Ethics by using that biased source without disclosing its nature and for becoming a central part of the story by manipulating David Stanley. I forgive him for covering up his lapses so he could qualify and win the prestigious Peabody Award.

I forgive Dale Hanson for embellishing his role in the SMU football scandal and lying to promote his career.

I forgive Sean Stopperich who solicited money from SMU boosters and then turned the school in for getting that money. Dead of a drug overdose at age twenty-nine.

I forgive David Stanley, for soliciting money from boosters to attend SMU. I forgive him for attempting to extort additional money to cover up those initial payments. I forgive him for his drug addiction and then for turning on SMU when they secretly paid for his drug rehab. Dead of a drug overdose at age thirty-nine.

I forgive Coach Bobby Collins, A.D. Bob Hitch, President L. Donald Shields, and the members of the SMU Board of Governors who knew about the payment fund for not having the strength to shut down the system in 1983 when they still had the chance.

I forgive the SMU football players who accepted payments. They were mainly poor kids without any financial support at home who accepted money to help cover the financial difference the NCAA has identified between scholarship benefits and the true cost of college.

I forgive the boosters who paid players at the request of SMU officials and thought they were helping the school they loved.

I forgive all these people, because we are all flawed and make mistakes. I forgive them because it has been twenty-five years and it is time to move on.

SMU has made great progress in the last few years rebuilding from the catastrophe that was the Death Penalty and forgiveness is the path forward from those times.

But there was this kid that did nothing wrong. He played by the rules, he worked out, he pursued his degree, and he tried to be a good football player. In his first three years at SMU he joined a fraternity and made great friends on and off the football field. He established a strong personal connection to the SMU community.

He was on his way to a successful football career and a successful academic career. That kid believed the NCAA when they told him that, "the educational experience of the student-athlete was paramount."

That kid was forced to choose between academics and athletics and then he was punished for choosing academics. That kid was forced to choose with no help and no contact from anybody at the NCAA.

I and my teammates didn't deserve that penalty. They penalized all of us for the actions of a few. I understand why they did it and I understand how they did it. I understand and I forgive them. But that kid, twenty-one-year-old Dave Blewett, does not.

The Bishop's Report

On campus the leaders of SMU requested the involvement of the United Methodist Church. That request resulted in "The Bishops' Committee Report on SMU" released June 1987. It outlined what happened and what needed to be done for SMU to recover from the scandal.

They resolved that the surest path to restoring Southern Methodist University's reputation was through a process of disclosure, repentance, reconciliation and renewal. They closed their report looking not to the past but to the future.

They requested that "creative steps should be taken to bring together all persons who were legitimately interested in SMU so that the efforts of everyone could be focused not on the problems of the past but on the opportunities and challenges of the future. A public event should be held...including participation of all of the constituencies of the University - past and present members of the Board of Trustees and Board of Governors, members of the College of Bishops, other clergy and lay leaders of the administration, faculty, staff, alumni, students and open to all members of the public - to demonstrate a visible drawing together of these persons interested in and concerned about SMU."

"The elements of repentance, reconciliation and renewal should be prominent in this event. Its focus should be on putting the past behind and articulating our vision of the future."

The event will "give an opportunity for the whole SMU community to put past sins behind symbolically and in the spirit of God who makes all things new, to celebrate a new beginning for a great academic institution related to The United Methodist Church."

Respectfully Submitted,

COMMITTEE OF BISHOPS

We never had this event and I think we should.

>>>

The Rocky Mountain News

DREAMS OF SMU'S GUILTLESS RUINED ALONG WITH THE GUILTY

By: Teri Thompson, Rocky Mountain News March 2, 1987

"They didn't give Dave Blewett a fancy car when he decided to play football for Southern Methodist University. They didn't set up a slush fund for him or give his mother a washing machine. He didn't arrive with a closet full of Guccis and silk shirts to help ease the pain of his transition from Cherry Creek High School to big-time college football. All they did for Dave Blewett was offer him a dream.

"I found out about SMU from some friends when I was a junior in high school," says Blewett, who graduated from Cherry Creek in 1984. "I'd hoped to get a chance to play there and dreamed of it. It was perfect for me. I came to a school that had everything I wanted. I love this school. Yeah, everything was perfect..."

It sits in ruins now.

When the NCAA announced last week that it would hit SMU with The Death Penalty – banning football for 1987 and limiting the Mustangs to only 7 road games in 1988 – Blewett's dream was over.

He is a Finance and Philosophy (double) major with a 3.3 grade-point average and he is having a hard time deciding if he wants to transfer to another school just for the sake of playing football. He is not alone.

All of SMU's players became eligible to transfer without having to sit out a year, but the question for most is the one

Blewett faces. He is a good player, but his future is probably in either finance or philosophy, not professional football, and he wonders if he would be hurting himself by leaving a very good school.

"I know I don't want to leave it behind," he says, "but for the last seven or eight years I've played football. I've got two years of eligibility left and I'm not sure I'm ready to give it up. There's a lot of talk about everybody leaving, but you have to sacrifice so much."

It is difficult for the football players to accept what has happened to them. Part of the reason is that most of them weren't involved in the scandal and part is that they know their team isn't the only one that operates illegally. "SMU was the same toward me when they recruited me as any of the other schools," says Blewett, who played defensive tackle for the Mustangs. "I'm biased, obviously, but I don't think it's fair they assess us the Death Penalty. It doesn't help clean up the program – it destroys it. Do you cut off your head when you have a headache?"

There are many unanswered questions about what happened to SMU. The schools violations are unquestioned, but for many of us the judgments seem to be flowing just a little too free and easy. It's not too hard to sit back and moralize about the actions of an institution that probably isn't that different from most we cheer on those pretty fall Saturdays.

That doesn't mean that what SMU did was right; it just means that the solutions to the problems in college football don't begin and end in Dallas. But the real tragedy, of course, is what has happened to the players. Blewett and his teammates have spent most of the past week worrying and talking and trying to figure out what to do about a situation over which they had little control. Their futures are, for the most part, in the hands of others. They're even going through the recruiting process again, being wooed and welcomed by the vultures that've descended upon their campus in search of strong bodies and quick feet.

"It's like high school all over again," says Blewett. "You can take five visits and all that, just like the first time. In a way it's good, though. It gives people a chance to play somewhere else, and you don't even have to get out the old phone numbers of the guys who recruited you."

Blewett doesn't know what he will do. Since the day last week when the team gathered around a closed-circuit television set in the locker room to receive its sentence, he has lived in a whirlwind of indecision. As soon as the NCAA said, "Let's do it," his life forever changed. "I never, ever imagined anything like this could happen," he says. "But I found out it can happen and it did happen. It happened to me."

Blewett swears he won't make the same mistake again. "It's a tough thing to take the rap for a few people," he says. "Every single player is paying for a few."

They are paying for those who got the cars...and the Guccis...and the money. The price was high. It was a nice kid's dream.

Acknowledgements and Sources

I could not have completed this book without the access and use of the tremendous volume of information that various sources provided.

The Internet was my main resource for data, source information, and opinion pieces. It is impossible to mention every source that I found. The Barking Carnival, SB Nation, Wikipedia and hundreds of other sites were hyper-linked as sources from Google search.

The main newspapers that I relied on were The Dallas Morning News, Houston Chronicle, and Wall Street Journal. I am grateful for various stories from their numerous reporters over a decade or more. The Rocky Mountain News, Los Angeles Times, and Dallas Times-Herald were also helpful.

A handful of books provided insights into the history of college football. Beer and Circus by Murray Sperber, College Football by John Watterson, and Unsportsmanlike Conduct by Walter Byers were detailed and reliable. An incredible article in the October 2011 issue of The Atlantic called The Shame of College Sports changed my entire view of the modern college athlete.

David Whitford's A Payroll to Meet along with The Bishops' Committee Report on SMU were the most useful relating to the specifics of SMU's interaction with the NCAA.

When it came time to understand the inner workings of the NCAA, Don Yeager's Undue Process and Andrew Zimbalist's Unpaid Professionals were invaluable.

Various issues and articles from Sports Illustrated about SMU and the NCAA from the 1970's and 1980's provided timely insights and detailed early conflicts.

The NCAA itself was a great source of material. I found numerous issues of The NCAA News with information that I couldn't find anywhere else. I utilized their Major Infractions Database for information regarding probations and penalties. The 1986 and 2011 editions of the NCAA Manuals provided an understanding of their rules.

There were many individuals that were helpful as friends, confidants, and supporters and I thank them. A partial list includes: John Wander, Greg Gardner, David Richards, Bobby Watters, Johnny Delavaldene, Joel Pechauer, Thaddeus Matula, Kevin Woltjen, Mike Shore, and of course friend and trainer extraordinaire Scott Snelgrove.

Lastly, my wife Kristin allowed me the time and space to complete this project. Thanks to her, I did it.

Printed in the USA
CPSIA information can be obtained
at www.ICGtesting.com
LVHW012023170124
768960LV00003B/99

9 780985 988302